Interchange Fee Economics

Jakub Górka

Interchange Fee Economics

To Regulate or Not to Regulate?

palgrave
macmillan

Jakub Górka
University of Warsaw
Warsaw, Poland

ISBN 978-3-030-03040-7 ISBN 978-3-030-03041-4 (eBook)
https://doi.org/10.1007/978-3-030-03041-4

Library of Congress Control Number: 2018959248

This Palgrave Macmillan imprint is published by the registered company Springer Nature Switzerland AG
The registered company address is: Gewerbestrasse 11, 6330 Cham, Switzerland

Contents

List of Figures

List of Tables

Introduction

The interchange fees have been, for many years now, the focal point for debate in the card industry, among competition authorities, policy makers as well as in the economic literature on two-sided markets and on the regulation of market failures (see e.g. works of Jean Tirole, the Noble Prize winner in Economic Sciences in 2014).

The book offers insight into the economics of interchange fees specific for four-party card schemes and explores the eternal question: *To Regulate, or Not to Regulate*? It discusses, from a multitude of perspectives, the effects of regulatory interchange fee reductions in various countries from all over the world. The discussion goes beyond the interchange fees and concentrates also on business rules, such as "no-honour-all-cards" or "no-surcharge" and other practices having impact on competition on the payment market and defending the market standing of the incumbent four-party card schemes, such as: reverse competition, blending, restrictions on access to schemes or on network switching.

The book's objective is to assess the costs and benefits of interchange fee regulations for all stakeholders: issuers, acquirers, card organisations, merchants and consumers. The general research question extends into more questions, for which answers are sought to better understand the intervention process and its outcome. What were the consequences of capping interchange fees for stakeholders, for competition, innovation and security of the payments market? What lessons can be drawn from the interchange fee reforms? Did all go as planned, with reforms bringing only the intended consequences? What were the positives and the negatives of the reforms in different countries? Is there a need to improve regulations or to regulate on an ongoing basis?

The study attempts to show implications of the dynamics of the impact of interchange fee regulations. For this purpose, an original framework is drawn up in Chapter 1. The framework addresses three areas of concern with respect to the transmission channels of interchange fee reductions (pass-through) and the card scheme domain:

- Area 1, transmission channel: acquirer → merchant → consumer (cardholder)
- Area 2, transmission channel: issuer → consumer (cardholder)
- Area 3, card scheme domain: payment organisation—issuer—acquirer

Area 1 considers network and monetary effects of the interchange fee decreases. Claim 1 and 2 describe causal mechanisms in accordance with the theory of two-sided markets. Lower interchange fees and corresponding merchant fees should result in broader card acceptance and intensified card usage. Claim 3 looks into the monetary effect, also consistent with the theory of two-sided markets, to examine whether savings from lower merchant fees are passed through by merchants in the form of lower prices for consumers. Area 2 focuses on the pass-through from issuers (banks) to consumers (cardholders). Claim 4 shows the flip side of the coin. Facing lower interchange fee revenues, issuers may try to raise card holder fees in order to keep profits the same. For the pass-through, competition in the issuer, acquirer and merchant markets is crucial. Consumer welfare depends on the magnitude of the monetary and network effects. The question is whether consumers gain more from the universality of cards and lower prices or they lose more from higher cardholder fees. What needs to be tested first, however, is whether the cardholder fee increases and the merchant price decreases take place or maybe the reality turns out more complex. Area 3 examines card organisations' policy adjustments coinciding with the interchange fee reforms. Claim 5 refers to the strategy of card organisations, which may see interchange fee reductions as neutral and choose not to redesign their scheme fees to compensate issuers for lower revenues at the expense of acquirers. However, the interchange fee reforms are likely to change market conditions and make issuers and other payment service providers more willing to innovate, develop cost-efficient payment instruments or support other payment solutions. The interchange fee reforms are set in the wider context of competition and innovation game.

Five claims are verified in Chapters 2 and 3 based on country cases. In Chapter 2 three country cases are investigated: Australia, USA, Spain. Chapter 3 examines the Polish case. All cases are interlinked with cross-section references. The book consists of three chapters in total. Each of the chapters has its own introduction briefly outlining its structure, and contains specific sections, where concise findings and key takeaways are given. Chapter 1 is more theoretical than Chapters 2 and 3, which are strictly empirical. Still, Chapter 1 is empirically oriented as well, since it gives multiple market examples and refers to the results of empirical studies when discussing various card payment issues.

Chapter 1 is divided in two parts. The first one introduces the theory of two-sided markets/networks/platforms that create value (indirect network effect) by connecting two distinct groups of agents, e.g. card payers and card payees. Such market settings exist in many sectors of the economy. This part characterises conditions defining two-sided markets and market failures which can arise there. It ends by listing threats to competition and countervailing factors on two-sided markets. The second part deals exclusively with economics of interchange fees and card payments. It explains the *modus operandi* of four- and three-party card schemes, their business model, inherent fees, and how they are set. It illuminates the role of interchange fees according to the classical Baxter's model and its later refinements in the economic literature, which extend Baxter's model to include heterogeneity of consumers and merchants or such phenomena as "business stealing" (also called "must-take-cards"), reverse competition or "single- and multi-homing". This part includes discussion of the optimal level of interchange fees maximising the joint welfare of consumers and merchants. There are different methods used to determine this level: a cost-based issuer approach and the merchant approach based on the "tourist test", developed by Rochet and Tirole and preferred lately, *inter alia* by the European Commission, for its better theoretical underpinnings. The tourist test applications for Poland, the Netherlands, the USA and the European Union are presented. Moreover, the discussion goes beyond the interchange fees and also centres around scheme business rules: "no-surcharge", "honour-all-cards" and the blending practice. The final paragraph of Chapter 1 develops the framework for assessing the impact of interchange fee regulation, which is used in Chapters 2 and 3.

Chapter 2 offers a truly global outlook on public authorities' involvement in card payments. It starts with elaborating on actions taken against interchange fee setting mechanism, against exaggerated fee levels or against anti-competitive scheme practices in France, EU (competition cases), Mexico, Canada, Israel, India and China. Then, Chapter 2 studies in detail, according to the framework from Chapter 1, three country cases: Australia, USA, Spain. This section concludes with a comparison of all three country cases summarising the impact of interchange fee reforms on: merchant service charges, card acceptance, card usage, prices, bank revenues and cardholder charges, four-party card schemes, competition and innovation. Different aspects of the reforms are discussed, including transparency measures. The last section of Chapter 2 describes the recent Interchange Fee Regulation in the European Union and its provisions. It is too early to evaluate its influence on the card payment market, but a few preliminary remarks can be made.

Chapter 3 is devoted entirely to the investigation of the Polish interchange fee reform, which is interesting for a number of reasons. *Primo*, Poland was the country with the highest average interchange fee rates in Europe. In 2014 they were decreased drastically by a regulatory act and then once again, at the beginning of 2015, before the Interchange Fee Regulation entered into force for all EU member states. *Secundo*, the impact assessment for the Polish reform is undertaken based on data from many sources as well as with the help of diversified methods comprising financial, econometric and legal analysis. After explaining the history of interchange fee reductions, Chapter 3 continues with demonstrating the results of two subsequent merchant surveys that draw a clear picture of the process of passing through interchange fee reductions from acquirers to merchants. Next, the analysis is developed according to the framework from Chapter 1. Claims 1 and 2 on the impact of interchange fee reductions on card acceptance and card usage are verified. Then, a close look is taken at bank interchange fee revenues, fee-based income and card- and accountholder fees (claim 4). The next section provides a unique, detailed and business-oriented study of Visa and Mastercard[1] scheme fees and their strategy at the time of interchange fee reforms (claim 5). This section goes deeper, showing implications of

[1]In line with 2016 logo and brand identity adjustments at Mastercard, the "Mastercard" spelling is used throughout the book rather than the previous one, "MasterCard".

the interchange fee reductions for competition, innovation and security on the Polish payment market. Finally, Chapter 3 ends with a summary section with a brief and clear recap of the impact assessment and a discussion of interchange fee reduction effects on the prices of goods and services in Poland (claim 3).

The last part, containing final remarks, reiterates some of the findings from Chapters 2 and 3 but more generally than in earlier summary sections. It links all the country cases studied. It addresses difficulties for public authorities in regulating interchange fees and card payments. Eventually, it gives recommendations for policy makers and stakeholders of the card and payments industry. The book puts the issue of interchange fees in the wider context of the entire payment system (innovation and competition, references to FinTechs, novel methods of payments, including digital wallets, bitcoins, real-time payments, etc.). There are examples from payment markets, references to the industry practice, and to other legal acts of paramount importance for the market such as the revised Payment Services Directive (PSD2) in the European Economic Area.

The book can be classified as literature on industrial organisation and financial economics. It is rooted in the theory of two-sided markets, but it constitutes an empirical study that, for Australian, American and Spanish country cases, relies partly on the findings of other researchers and central banks and partly on the author's own calculations and deduction. The analysis is, however, original and developed according to the framework for assessing the impact of interchange fee regulations from Chapter 1. Chapter 3 as a whole is the author's empirical work where different research methods are used, ranging from financial, legal and business analysis to sophisticated econometric modelling. In the book, the author relies mainly on public databases of central banks and supervisors, publicly available information of card schemes and banks, and on business and research reports. Chapter 1 contains an extensive literature study that helps understand the interchange fee economics, and further empirical studies developed in Chapters 2 and 3.

The author builds on his rich experience and expertise in the field, i.e. on:

- his research projects (he was three times the principal investigator of the research projects aimed at examining various aspects of interchange fee economics, including measurement of the pass-through rate of interchange fee reductions from acquirers to merchants or the investigation of costs of card and cash acceptance for the purpose of tourist test application in the joint research project of the National Bank of Poland (NBP), Foundation For Development of Cashless Payments (FROB) and the Faculty of Management, University of Warsaw (FoM UW); earlier on, he was investigator in several other research projects on payments),

- his experience from consulting and preparing expert opinions for the National Bank of Poland, the Polish Ministry of Finance, Foundation For Development of Cashless Payments, commercial companies engaged in the card business,
- his experience as the European Commission's expert on payments (since 2012 he has been a member of the Payment Systems Market Expert Group assisting the European Commission in preparing legislation and policy initiatives for payment issues).

The book precedes the impact study of the Interchange Fee Regulation in the European Union which—according to the review clause—will have to be published by the European Commission in mid-2019. The studies and conclusions from this book may be of value for the European Commission and for all the parties interested in the modalities of the interchange fee economics. The target audience is policy makers, card and payments industry people, academics and students.

The author wants to thank all those who have helped him in his studies by providing consultation, assistance and comments or simply wished him good luck with succeeding in publication.

CHAPTER 1

Two-Sided Markets and Interchange Fees

This chapter consists of two parts. Part I describes two-sided markets, thus providing the background knowledge needed to understand the implications of four-party card schemes formed in a two-sided network. Part II deals with interchange fees in card payments. Interchange fees as well as other fees applicable in four-party card schemes are thoroughly discussed.

1.1 Introduction to Two-Sided Markets

This part introduces the concept of two-sided markets, also called two-sided platforms or two-sided networks in the economic and information technology literature. Section 1.1.1 shows the value of platforms connecting specific groups of agents having interrelated interests. Two-sided platforms utilise indirect network effects. Section 1.1.2 gives multiple examples of two-sided platforms from different sectors of economy. It explains the business model and the pricing policy of platforms. This section sets out conditions defining two-sided markets. Section 1.1.3 addresses market imperfections which can arise in two-sided markets and make regulators act in defence of consumers and competition.

1.1.1 Indirect Network Effects in Two-Sided Platforms

The power of competition in a free market economy is based on the scale of interactions between entities. Trade in real economy benefits from the high number of sellers and buyers of goods and services. Similarly, free

J. Górka, *Interchange Fee Economics*,
https://doi.org/10.1007/978-3-030-03041-4_1

flow of capital in financial markets depends critically on the number of investors buying and selling securities in a free float. By matching buyers and sellers, platforms improve the market mechanism, because their operations reduce traditional transaction costs as defined by Williamson (2010). Platforms contribute to the ease of interactions, to lower search and bargaining costs and may decrease information asymmetries. A concentration of sellers and buyers can lead to lower prices and a greater overall efficiency of the system for the flow of goods and capital.

Many markets on which network externalities occur are classified as two-sided or even multi-sided markets. On two-sided markets, the interaction between two separate groups of entities takes place on a platform that serves as an intermediary and service provider. Entities of one group benefit from contacts with entities of the other group. The larger both groups and subsequently interactions (transactions) between both groups, the greater so-called indirect network effect, not to be confused with the direct network effect specific for interactions within a group, which is not a determinant of a two-sided market (Katz and Shapiro 1985).

The value of Android operating system has for its users comes from the number of apps offered by the developers on Google Play Store. The latter write apps for Android mobile platform because they hope to see their products reach many users. The larger both groups of entities, the greater the indirect network effect, i.e. the perceived value of Android platform among those writing and using native apps. Android also enables communication between app users, who can rate them, thus informing other people about their experience. Mutual communication and app rating represent a direct network effect, which has a positive impact on its value, but—as mentioned before—is not the essence of the two-sided market. The essence in this particular case is matching developers and users. Apple's iOS operates exactly the same as Android, even if it forms a more closed ecosystem. Android and iOS are two global competing mobile platforms. They currently operate in duopoly and dominate the smartphone market. Payment apps of banks and non-bank FinTech (Financial Technology) innovative companies are written for those two mobile operating systems. Figure 1 schematically presents the concept of a two-sided market.

In two-sided markets the demands of two groups of agents (entities) are interdependent. There can be usage or membership externalities.

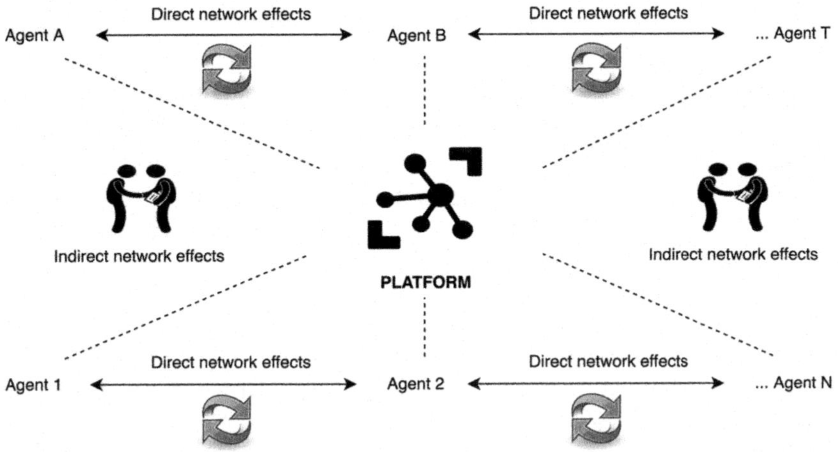

Fig. 1 Concept of a two-sided market. *Note* Agent A, B, …T—group one of agents (e.g. sellers); Agent 1, 2, …N—group two of agents (e.g. buyers) (*Source* Own compilation)

Payment card users care about the size of merchant acceptance network, not about how many card transactions merchants accept. In contrast, merchants prefer to join a card network in which cardholders actually use cards. From merchants' perspective, what matters is card usage, not membership alone (Rysman 2009: 126).

The theory of two-sided markets assumes that a platform's utility depends on the number of network members on the other side of the market (indirect network effect). Consequently, if a platform attracts n_1 entities in the first group and n_2 entities in the other one, the utility of group 1 entity (u_1) and of group 2 entity (u_2) can be expressed as follows (Armstrong 2006: 672):

$$u_1 = \alpha_1 n_2 - p_1$$
$$u_2 = \alpha_2 n_1 - p_2$$

where p_1 and p_2 are prices charged by the platforms to both sides of the market, while α_1 and α_2 are parameters measuring the marginal benefit group 1 entity reaps from the interaction with group 2 entity (or conversely).

1.1.2 Business Model and Pricing Policy

Economists pay special attention to the platforms' pricing policy. As observed by Rochet and Tirole (2003), and by many other economists who study this topic (e.g. Wright 2004a; Evans and Schmalensee 2005; Armstrong 2006; Hagiu and Hałaburda 2014), a two-sided market is one where the number and value of transactions depend on the structure and level of fees charged to both sides of the market. In a two-sided market, where indirect network effects occur, usually the price elasticity of demand varies between both groups of platform users. Therefore, one of them is charged transaction fees while the other one is provided with service below the marginal costs, and often incurs no transaction fees. In addition, the platform may charge both groups fixed fees for access to its services (membership/access fees). If entities from both groups are capable of internalising the indirect network effects by coordinating mutual activities, the two-sided market becomes a one-sided market. Rochet and Tirole (2006: 11–12) show that the four-party card payment system with an interchange fee can become one-sided when:

- charges and benefits are passed through by issuers and acquirers to merchants and consumers,
- merchants charge to consumers two different prices for cash and card payments,
- merchants and consumers incur no transaction costs due to the system of double prices.

Platforms implement strategies to increase the indirect network effects, that is interactions between agents of the two distinct groups. Characteristic for two-sided markets is that a platform seeks to reap financial benefits from the fees imposed on one side (profit centre) whereas the other side of the market is subsidised (loss centre). Table 1 presents examples of such pricing strategy in various branches of economy.

A platform may charge fees both for access (membership) and for use, that is for every interaction between users of both network sides. Many two-sided markets involve a situation where a business transaction is concluded through a platform between buyer (B–buyer) and seller (S–seller). This is the case of online auction sites (Amazon, eBay, Allegro, etc.) or of real estate agencies. However, there are two-sided markets such as media markets, on which no business transaction is directly concluded through

Table 1 Business model examples on two-sided markets

Market example	*Subsidised market side (loss centre)*	*Profit-yielding side (profit centre)*
Media		
Television	Viewers	Advertisers
Newspapers	Readers	Advertisers
Web portals	Users	Advertisers
Software		
Operating systems (Android, iOS, Windows)	App developers	Users
PDF creators and readers	Users of read-only versions (e.g. Acrobat Reader)	Users of read-write versions (e.g. Adobe Acrobat)
Payment Systems		
Card payment systems (Visa, Mastercard, American Express, Diners Club)	Cardholders	Merchants
Retail and Intermediation		
Shopping centres	Customers	Shops
Online auction sites (Amazon, eBay, Allegro, etc.)	Buyers	Sellers
Deal aggregators (coupon books or coupon apps)	Consumers	Shops
Real estate agencies	Buyers	Sellers

Source Own compilation

a platform. Television viewers do not buy advertised products from the screen, and neither do readers of newspapers and web portals (though on the internet web portal users can click on the link, be redirected to the electronic shop in an instant and make a purchase). In media, advertisers are the side that pays greater attention to the size of a medium's audience. For the latter, the number of advertisements does not have to necessarily involve greater value. Viewers pay the price by being compelled to watch advertisements. The advertisers' presence makes the business case for the platform.

As concerns news web portals, a user interested in the portal's content becomes, willy-nilly, the target of advertising for which portals get paid by advertisers. On the other hand, the user, through the portal, has access to rich content and to many services—e.g. electronic mail, virtual drive, chat, video on demand, games, etc. Many of those services, in their standard version, are offered to users free of charge by the platform (including articles and news classified by topics), but some of them are paid (e.g. premium mail, some games and videos).

The purpose of the platform is to get both sides on board. The more users there are on both sides of the market, the greater utility the platform offers. It targets the needs and provides diverse services to both groups. The fee structure and level may contain not only variable components but also fixed ones. Assuming there are no fixed membership fees for accessing a platform connecting buyers and sellers, the following example of a platform which charges transaction fees, a^B and a^S, respectively, to both sides of the market can be considered (Rochet and Tirole 2006):

$$a^A = a^B + a^S$$

$$V = f\left(a^B, a^S\right)$$

The total price (a^A) charged by the platform is the sum of prices a^B and a^S. If the number of transactions (interactions) V depends solely on the aggregated price level (a^A), and the price reallocation between buyers and sellers is of no consequence to it, the market is one-sided. On the other hand, if the number of transactions varies depending, for example, on a^B and meanwhile a^A is *constant*, then we're dealing with a two-sided market. Empirical research serves to indicate which side on a given market has a higher price elasticity of demand, and which side a lower one, and, consequently, which one should be subsidised or charged to bring profits. In accordance with the concept of two-sided markets, a change in the pricing structure depending on which side of the market is charged transaction fees has an impact on the platform's overall efficiency, i.e. on its utility (number of interactions) and cost efficiency.

No price being imposed on one side of the market should not be the reason to deny the fact that such a market exists (Evans 2003; Filistrucchi et al. 2014). It is economically necessary to take account of the other side of the market. The role of the platform is to lead to an effective matching of both parties ("getting both sides on board"). The pricing strategy should be tailored and in some cases it requires more than providing a service to one side of the market at a price that is lower than marginal costs; the price may be zero or even, in an extreme case, set at a negative level. Then a platform actually subsidises and pays or rewards a group of users.

A canonical example of a two-sided market is offered by nightclubs for heterosexual clients. Wright (2004a) uses this example to describe eight fallacies as regards the evaluation of a platform's pricing policy, which can be committed when using the logic of a classical approach to two-sided markets.

The example analysed by Wright (2004a) and Evans and Schmalensee (2005, 2007) mostly referred to the 1990s and early twenty-first century. Back then nightclubs and discos encouraged men and women to party together by offering women free entrance to the club (price $=0$) or women would even receive a free cocktail at the door (price < 0, direct subsidy), while men had to pay for entering the club, quite a lot at times. Moreover, while partying at the club men were much more often the side buying expensive cocktails and drinks at a price that greatly exceeded their marginal cost for the club. Women were the side subsidised by the platform, while men, the side subsidising the platform. However, such a pricing strategy used by a club/discotheque was accepted by both sides as it was conducive to the desirable interaction. Men benefited from the fact that a lot of women were partying at the club, while women, from the presence of many partying men. The service offered by the platform consisted in making it possible to spend time together with music. Club managers were right in how they identified price elasticity of women and men. The latter were a side that was more willing to spend money, so clubs' income came from them. Men were charged a cover fee (fixed access fee) and for drinks (variable transaction fee).

Shopping centres cater to sellers who rent space at the centre, and to consumers—customers of shops located within its space. Indirectly, the volume of customer traffic at the centre, and directly the number of sales transactions concluded are the measure of the shopping mall's value. However, its scope of services to both groups is different. What a shopping centre offers to shops, against payment, is space of varied size, which may have a more or less attractive location within the facility. Moreover, the centre sells to shops a positioning service in the form of promoting their products (leaflets, stickers, advertising banners, etc.). Consumers are the group that is usually provided by the shopping mall, free of charge, with a number of facilities, from free entry, to free parking, to a free leisure opportunity in nice surroundings. Placing many shops of different categories is an advantage to customers who reduce their transaction costs (time and transport expenses) by visiting one location.

It follows from the above discussion that a two-sided market/platform exists when three conditions are met:

1. There are two separate groups of entities between which an indirect network effect can be identified, i.e. there is a need for interaction which benefits both sides.
2. A platform is in place which causes the indirect network effect to be internalised by both groups of entities. A platform provides services adapted to each side of the market, which supplement the core benefit that is the possibility of an interaction between them (on transactional market the interaction is tantamount to selling/buying goods or services).
3. The volume of transactions depends on reallocation of the total price between two sides of the market. If demand, rather than being dependent on the aggregated price, varies depending on the structure of the prices charged to both sides of the market, the third premise is met. In accordance with the adopted logic of two-sided markets, it is justified to make a profit on one group of entities while making a loss on another group of entities.

1.1.3 Regulators' Concern About Market Failure

The value of a platform lies in enabling contact between both sides of the market. Oftentimes, if it were not for a platform's operations, effective trade would not be possible or it would be greatly hindered. However, platforms can also operate in a way that restricts competition and harms consumers. Regulators and antitrust offices must be vigilant about any market failure due to platforms' activities. Frequently the major concern for regulators is the pricing policy/strategy used by the platform, but there are also other issues which may infringe competition, such as, e.g. market power resulting from market concentration, high entry barriers or anti-competitive practices like bundling and tying of products.

As demonstrated, the economic interdependence between two sides of the market implicates *modus operandi* of the platform and its pricing strategy, which may provide for catering to one group of entities below the marginal costs. The platform may take profit from fees charged to the other side of the market. The task of the antitrust authorities should be to verify whether the fees charged to any side of the market are reasonable and include no economic rent (Evans and Noel 2008; Börestam and Schmiedel 2011). One of such cases, discussed in detail in next sections and chapters, are four-party card schemes which make use of interchange fees.

The market power of a platform can be limited when it is subject to a market pressure. If a user (e.g. buyer—compare Fig. 2) can use services of several platforms (multi-home) to satisfy needs of a given type, then the market power of each of them is generally lower as they compete for the same client when offering similar products. Therefore, what matters for the competitiveness of two-sided markets, is the user's ability to use other substitute platforms rather than just one, i.e. multi-home instead of single-home (Caillaud and Jullien 2003; Rochet and Tirole 2003; Doganoglu and Wright 2006; Hagiu and Jullien 2014; Belleflamme and Toulemonde 2016).

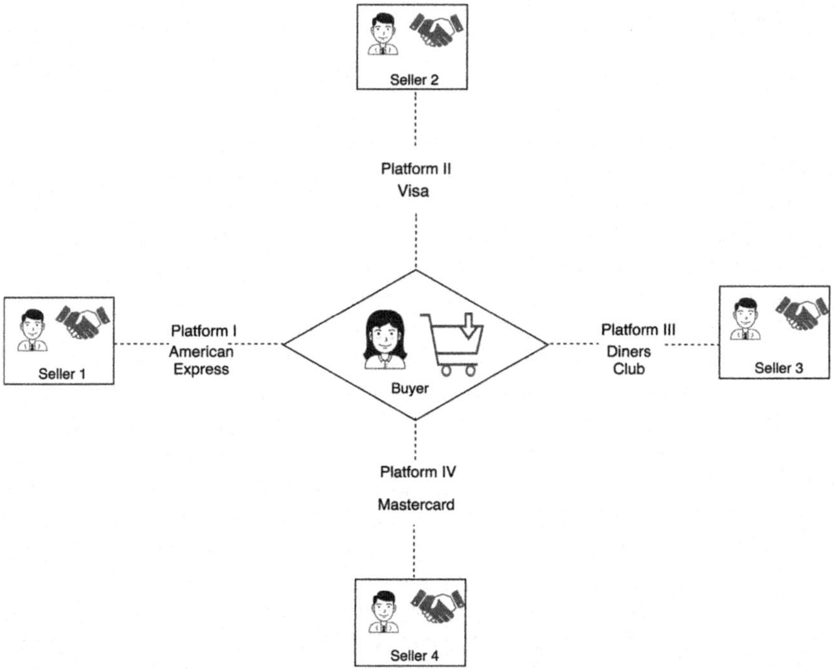

Fig. 2 Multi-homing in card payments (*Source* Own compilation)

As regards payment cards, the competition is between payment systems Visa, Mastercard, American Express, Diners Club, as well as between cash payment and mobile payment systems—e.g. Blik in Poland, MobilePay in Denmark, WeChat Pay in China. Consumers may choose a payment instrument that best suits their preferences as long as it's accepted by a given shop (multi-homing). Each of payment instruments equally well satisfies the main need, i.e. enables a payment transaction and a sale of goods.

Another example of multi-homing, which has an impact on the competition level, are shopping centres. Consumers can go to different shopping malls and thus multi-home. Besides, sellers may offer their products not only at shopping centres but also through their own websites, standalone outlets, auction online sites or points of sale located in supermarket shopping arcades. A buyer may use many channels of distribution, where prices of the same product may be and usually are different. In all likelihood, two of those channels of distribution meet the criteria of a platform—online auction sites and shopping arcades in supermarkets. In the example quoted, direct sales at a brick-and-mortar outlet and a shop's online sales are a one-sided market.

Tying and bundling of products are usually treated as practices limiting customer choice and inflating customer costs. On two-sided markets they can deliver value (Evans and Schmalensee 2005, 2007) and at the same time give rise to negative externalities, e.g. the honour-all-cards rule in card payment systems benefits cardholders but also forces merchants to accept expensive cards whose cost is in turn passed through by merchants to consumers in the form of higher prices. Choi (2010) argues that the negative impact of tying can be limited or completely eliminated, when consumers multi-home. Their welfare could even enhance but in the absence of multi-homing the welfare impact of tying would be negative.

From the perspective of potential threats to competition resulting from concentrations of undertakings, it is of importance to assess whether and to what degree the following will increase: market power of a merged entity and market entry barriers. In this context, we talk of so-called horizontal and vertical effects of merger on two-sided markets (TILEC 2010: 122). Evans and Noel (2008) demonstrate that the traditional methods for evaluating mergers between companies operating on one-sided markets may lead to wrong conclusions, if applied to two- or multi-sided markets. In a correct analysis, one should take into account the indirect network effect between two (or more) sides of the market, and, consequently, the change in the price of services at both sides. As much as a comprehensive analysis of both market sides in the process of evaluating platform consolidation has its merits, it is worth bearing in mind the practical difficulties involved, especially *ex ante*. Moreover, one should exercise great caution when defining the breadth of the relevant product market because this is what the future conclusions mostly hinge on. When it comes to web portals, it matters whether only the largest news portals or many lesser dedicated services, as well, are taken into account. As concerns shopping malls, the conclusions will be quite different if we consider all of the shops' sales channels. Meanwhile, for payment cards, what matters is whether the relevant market is defined in the most narrow way as a four-party payment card market or more broadly as a market for four-party and three-party payment cards or yet more broadly as a market for cashless payment instruments, or in the most broad way as a payment market.

As regards the market power and the attendant possible increase in service prices, the European Commission, when analysing mergers of two global distribution systems (GDS), took note of several factors that limit the market power of the entities being merged—Travelsport and Worldspan (European Commission 2007). The GDSs operate on the tourism market. They are systems for electronic distribution of information on prices and products of different tourism service providers, i.e. airlines, hotels, car rentals. Global distribution systems share this information with travel agencies and travel operators who, on behalf of a client, can make a relevant booking, buy a ticket or purchase another service. Travel agencies search for and compare different companies' offers. GDSs earn on fees charged to providers depending on the number and value of products sold through the platform (e.g. tickets for airlines). Travel agencies bear fixed costs of integration with a given GDS. Providers of products and services are interested to be present on each GDS platform, which is why it is enough for a travel agency to connect to one platform. When evaluating the merger of Galileo (Travelsport) and Worldspan platforms, the platform's ability to increase the price was analysed. However, it turned out that there was hardly any as the providers still had a high bargaining power. Airlines and other providers were able to select the scope of services provided to a given platform, i.e. for example cheap tickets would be removed from a platform increasing the price of tickets, and placed on competitive platforms as well as offered by own sales channel. Moreover, airlines were able to impose surcharges on tickets sold by a given platform, which would consequently increase the price for travel agency, and then for the travel agency's client (consumer).

As concerns market entry barriers, it is worth quoting the words of 2014 Nobel prize winner in economics, Jean Tirole, who received it, among other things, in recognition of his achievements in the development of game and two-sided market theory for the purposes of regulation of monopolies and oligopolies. When the Swedish central bank's awarding committee's decision was announced, he was asked how his theories could be applied to evaluate the market position of companies such as Google. Tirole replied that in some branches of economy there is a natural tendency to create monopolies but it's not a problem as long as monopolists can be replaced with new companies. The possibility of market entry must be ensured to allow new, innovative and dynamically growing companies to take over market share from dominant companies (compare Tirole 2014).

However, a common problem is the lock-in, or a situation where a given solution or system becomes a market standard, whose value results from a strong network effect. Then new players have difficulties selling their product, even if it is cheaper and better than the one widespread on the market (Liebowitz and Margolis 1995; Arthur 1999; Górka 2009: Chapter 5). A good example would be the social media and social networking market with a globally dominant share of Facebook. Another example could be Microsoft Windows platform as an operating system for desktops and laptops. The growing number of users and developers who operate on the platform increases associated network effects. Competitive products are not able to gain market share from the dominant rival, even if they offer, in some respects, a higher functionality of their product. So-called switching or moving to a competitive platform depends on the network effect and on how high the transaction costs are, including the time invested in learning and adapting to new platform (e.g. new operating system or new social networking service).

Closely related to the network effect and to the lock-in is the problem of critical mass or chicken-and-egg deadlock. Some time ago it affected digital wallet systems (e.g. ChipKnip in the Netherlands and Proton in Belgium). Sellers would not invest in terminals adapted to processing payments with electronic money stored on special microchip cards, as they were afraid their investment would not pay off, the group of electronic wallets being too small. Meanwhile, consumers were not willing to use the new form of money as the merchant base was no sufficiently

Table 2 Threats to competition and countervailing forces on two-sided markets—synthesis

Threats to competition	*Countervailing forces*
• Platform's market power resulting in the ability to dictate a price on one or both sides of the market (potentially much above the sum total of marginal costs incurred by the platform) • Ability to use anti-competition practices by the platform such as tying, bundling, ban on one side of the market imposing additional fees on the other (ban on surcharge) • Market concentration of platforms through mergers and acquisitions • High market entry barriers and strong network effect: - Chicken-and-egg deadlock - Lock-in effect	• Multi-homing • Diversified sales channels • Bargaining power of one of the market sides • Possibility for both sides to internalise the network effect through coordinated actions, including through unbundling of the platform's services • Possibility of one side of the market (seller) granting rewards, offering rebates or imposing fees (surcharge) on the other (buyer) without the platform's consent • Low transaction costs when switching between platforms • Quality of a new platform which satisfies user needs much better

Source Own compilation

extensive and debit and credit cards, and cash, all characterised by strong network effects, were in parallel use. Consequently, consumers and sellers were able to use popular payment instruments (platforms), so it was hard to convince them to use the new means of payment (Van Hove 1999).

Table 2 summarises threats to competition and countervailing factors on two-sided markets. Below, in the next part of this chapter and in subsequent chapters the discussion will exclusively focus on card payments and on the impact of interchange fee caps on domestic payment markets. Regulators in many countries found interchange fees to be excessive and saw them as a result of market failure.

1.2 Interchange Fees in Card Payments

This part presents the economics of interchange fees. Section 1.2.1 elaborates on four-party card schemes and compares them with three- and two-party schemes. It explains the interchange fee and other fees in the four-corner model: scheme, consumer and merchant fees, respectively. Section 1.2.2 focuses on the rationale behind interchange fees based on the classical Baxter's model from 80s. It also clarifies the assumptions of the model. Section 1.2.3 shows the development of Baxter's model in the literature and discusses practices and forces shaping the four-party card schemes, such as, e.g. "business stealing", reverse competition and multi-homing, which affect the welfare of both sides of the payment market: consumers and merchants. Following works of Rochet and Tirole this section introduces the "tourist test" as, arguably, the best method for determining the optimum level of interchange fees. It shows and discusses the results of the "tourist test" application for Poland, the Netherlands, the USA and the European Union. Section 1.2.4 delves deeper into analysing the significance of the scheme business rules ("no-surcharge", "honour-all-cards") and the blending practice. This part is concluded by Sect. 1.2.5 presenting the original framework for assessing the impact of regulatory interchange fee caps for its participants: consumers, merchants, acquirers, issuers and card organisations. Three areas are addressed with reference to the transmission channels of interchange fee reductions. Five claims are formulated that will be investigated in two subsequent chapters, comprising the empirical investigation of interchange fee reductions' pass-through and their broader effects.

1.2.1 Interchange Fee and Other Fees in Four-Party Card System

In four-party card schemes (such as Visa and Mastercard) an interchange fee is paid by the acquirer to the issuer (Fig. 3). Acquirers charge merchants a transaction fee, called a merchant service charge (MSC) or merchant discount. Consumers purchase goods and services with their payment cards, most typically not being aware of the fee paid by the merchant for the card payment. Merchant discounts (including interchange fees) are incorporated in the price of merchandise sold to consumers, unless merchants surcharge them for card transactions.

The four-party model can be linked with the theory of two-sided markets. In many industries, including the payment card industry, platforms cater to two (or more) groups of users and facilitate interactions between them (Evans and Schmalensse 2007). Attracting both sides to the platform requires that each side is charged adequately (Wright 2004a). Skewed pricing is prevalent. In card payments, the platform makes more revenues on the merchant side, because retailers exhibit a lower price elasticity than cardholders (Rochet and Tirole 2002).

Open-loop four-party payment schemes owe their success to a scalable non-transparent business model, in which an interchange fee is an

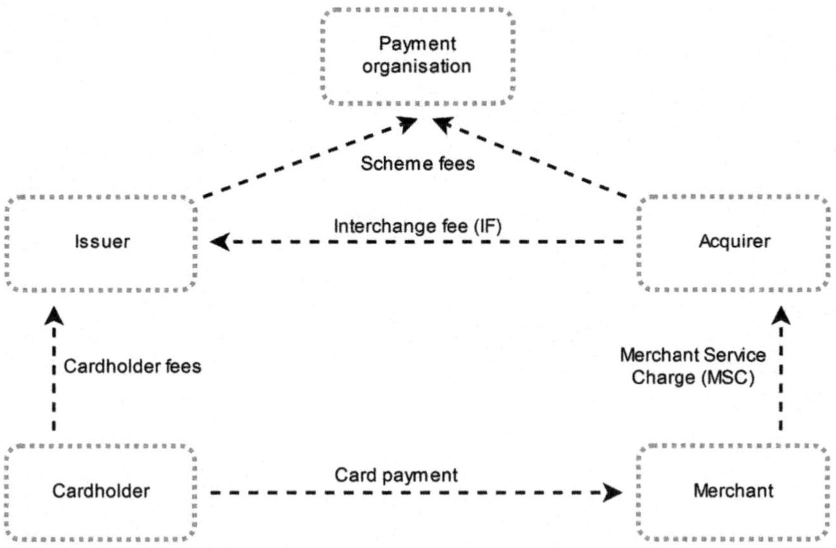

Fig. 3 Fee-setting in the four-party card scheme with an interchange fee (*Source* Own compilation)

inherent component of the structure of fees and charges. According to the working principle of the card scheme, interchange fees, together with merchant service charges, serve to balance the demands of cardholders (consumers) and merchants in order to maximise the number and value of card payments. The interchange fee mechanism contributes to enhancing indirect network effects. It is assumed that issuers incur higher costs (processing, payment guarantee, production, promotion) and are subject to higher risks (fraud, credit risk, etc.) than acquirers (Börestam and Schmiedel 2011). Therefore, in compliance with Visa and Mastercard rules, the interchange fee revenue for card payments flows from acquirers to issuers (for ATM transactions it goes in the opposite direction). The interchange fee thus serves as a balancing mechanism, with the acquiring side compensating for higher costs and risks of the issuing side.

Note that nowadays issuers and acquirers do not have to be banks. Prior to the first Payment Services Directive in Europe, it was not so uncommon for providers from outside the banking sector to run an acquiring business. After the law came into force (with delay in some member states), non-banking acquiring intensified. In addition, newly licensed non-bank payment service providers obtained the right to qualify for issuing Visa and Mastercard branded cards as international card schemes adjusted their rules to the law in Europe and to industry dynamics globally. While banks are still the dominant card issuers, non-bank FinTechs are making inroads into their payments business.

In addition to four-party schemes there are also closed-loop schemes with three or two parties. In three-party schemes, a payment organisation performs the functions of issuer and acquirer at the same time. Well-known three-party schemes are Diners Club and American Express. In the most simple configuration, there are only two parties in the system. A retailer can issue a card and accept it in its own network of shops, thus acquiring and settling all payment transactions within its closed environment.

Interchange fees can be set multilaterally or bilaterally. Historically, banks found bilateral interchange fee setting cumbersome and effort-intensive because of the number of one-to-one negotiations that would have to take place in a given country. Therefore, they preferred multilateral interchange fees. This method of price setting concerned competition authorities. They have long feared that collective decisions made by banks or by the scheme itself acting for the sake of issuers (member banks) might cause fee levels to be higher than necessary. The argument behind such reasoning is that interchange fees generate revenues for issuing banks, so these have a vested interest in elevating their rate. Currently, if not regulated, interchange fees are determined directly by international card schemes. POS and ATM interchange fees in pricing tables of Mastercard and Visa can be called reimbursement fees, fallback rates or collection rates. In practice, detailed tables can be quite complex because card schemes may differentiate their rates depending on:

- geography (domestic/intra-country/inter-country fees),
- type of card (debit/credit, consumer/business, magnetic stripe/EMV, etc.)
- type of transaction (card present/card-not-present),
- type of merchant (sector of activity, e.g. airline, government, wholesale),
- etc.

Table 3 gives an overview of weighted average (multilateral) interchange fee (MIF) rates for the countries of the European Economic Area as of December 2012 for Mastercard and Visa debit and credit cards. There are noticeable differences in levels among countries. Cyprus, Czech Republic and in particular Poland stand out, with the highest fees (up to circa 1.6%). Usually, swipe fees for credit cards are set higher than for debit cards. According to European Commission estimates

Table 3 Weighted average MIF rates in EEA countries in December 2012 (in %)

Country	*Mastercard debit MIF (%)*	*Mastercard credit MIF (%)*	*Visa debit MIF (%)*	*Visa credit MIF (%)*
Austria	NA	NA	1.00	1.00
Belgium	0.31	0.91	0.19	0.65
Bulgaria	NA	NA	0.48	0.48
Cyprus	NA	NA	**1.50**	**1.50**
Czech Republic	**1.23**	**1.20**	**1.21**	**1.21**
Denmark	NA	NA	0.30	0.75
Estonia	0.66	0.70	1.00	1.00
Finland	0.45	NA	0.19	0.65
France	0.55	0.58	0.52	0.44
Germany	0.48	NA	0.59	**1.63**
Greece	0.75	**1.29**	0.57	1.00
Hungary	0.71	0.98	0.19	0.65
Iceland	0.71	0.91	0.19	0.65
Ireland	0.22	0.91	0.28	0.72
Italy	0.52	0.82	0.48	0.65
Latvia	0.68	0.84	0.19	0.55
Liechtenstein	NA	NA	1.02	1.02
Lithuania	1.07	1.10	1.06	1.06
Luxembourg	0.37	0.91	0.19	0.65
Malta	0.71	0.91	0.1	0.65
Netherlands	0.29	0.91	0.19	0.65
Norway	0.67	1.15	0.40	1.00
Poland	**1.59**	**1.54**	**1.66**	**1.48**
Portugal	NA	NA	1.02	**1.48**
Romania	1.18	1.30	1.20	1.20
Slovakia	NA	NA	0.70	0.70
Slovenia	0.71	0.91	**1.27**	**1.27**
Spain	NA	NA	0.64	0.79
Sweden	0.47	0.91	0.19	0.65
UK	0.22	0.86	0.27	0.90
Intra-EEA	0.20	0.30	0.20	0.55

Note Rates of 1.20% and higher are in bold
Source European Commission (2013) *Staff Working Document (Impact assessment for PSD2 and IF Regulation)*, SWD 288

(European Commission 2013: 122) revenues from MSCs in the EU amounted to around EUR 14 billion annually, out of which about 70%, or EUR 10 billion, was transferred in interchange fees to issuers. A significant share of this figure was produced by credit cards and expensive premium cards.

Payment organisations themselves do not receive any direct revenue from interchange fees (see Fig. 3) but they collect scheme (assessment, network) fees collected from issuing and acquiring institutions. There is a variety of scheme fees. They are charged for issuing cards (licence fees), for transaction processing and for marketing purposes. Some of them are fixed, some are variable. Visa and Mastercard favour issuers and acquirers that report high volume of transactions. In effect, variable fees linked to the number and value of transactions are typically tiered and degressive (the higher the value, the fewer basis points are transferred to Visa and Mastercard).

International card organisations are free to decide about rules and fees in their systems. Effective governance of issuers and acquirers contributes to the global success of cards bearing the logo of international card organisations. Mastercard and Visa spend considerable amount of money on promoting non-cash payments and their payment networks. Their brands enjoy high trust and excellent publicity worldwide. Member banks and other member or affiliated institutions must strictly obey organisational rules and pay the non-negotiable price in scheme fees, which are not low. Their level and structure are reviewed and changed periodically. Visa and Mastercard make high profits. As publicly traded companies on the New York Stock Exchange, they have to disclose financial statements. For the fiscal year 2016 ending on 30 September 2016, Visa Inc. reported USD 15 billion total operating revenues and almost USD 6 billion net income, whereas for the fiscal year ending on 31 December 2016, Mastercard reported nearly USD 11 billion net revenues and USD 4 billion net income. Visa Inc. went public in 2008 raising a record USD 17.9 billion and Mastercard two years earlier raising USD 5.3 billion. In 2016, Visa Inc. acquired its European sister organisation Visa Europe, creating one single global company.

Interchange fees or swipe fees are used in four-corner schemes regardless of the type of card: prepaid, debit or credit (possibly charge). However, banks adjust their pricing policy to each of the card types, taking into account its specifics. Cardholders can be charged issuing fees. There may be a charge for the reissuing of a stolen or lost card.

Cardholders can be charged a fixed monthly fee for a debit card or a fixed annual fee for a credit card. Banks can also levy other card fees on their clients. Some of cardholder fees, most often associated with debit cards, are bundled with fees for current bank accounts.

Banks may attach additional benefits to credit cards, but increasingly also to debit cards. Cardholders can earn loyalty rewards (e.g. air miles) or other bonuses, such as rebates for dining and entertainment or discounts at shops. Sometimes cardholders can receive money back on their card spending, e.g. 1%. Money (or cash) back programmes tend to be more widespread at times when, and in countries where interchange fee rates are set higher. Then, banks are more ready to share their card issuing profits with clients who actively use their cards for purchases.

Credit card payments result in debt as another source of income for issuers, affecting their pricing policy. If cardholders do not clear their debt within the grace period, they must bear interest charges and possibly pay other fees (e.g. associated with an undue payment or with reminders about their debt clearing obligation).

Merchant pay merchant service charges (MSCs) to acquirers on a transaction basis. In addition, they usually pay a fixed fee for renting a payment terminal and possibly some other fees, e.g. for chargebacks or for service better tailored to their needs. MSCs can take form of a percentage fee or a combined fee. The latter includes both a percentage and a flat fee component. A single MSC, not differentiated among card types, is called blended.

The level of scheme fees is more transparent to merchants if they pay non-blended merchant service charges to acquirers in the interchange fee plus plus (IF++) structure. In such a case, a merchant discount attributed to a specific card consists of three components: an interchange fee, a scheme (processing) fee and an acquiring fee (an acquiring margin).

Table 4 shows the industry pricing framework for merchant discounts. A blended fee is the simplest formula. Its downside for merchants is that they are not aware of underlying fees and cannot distinguish between cheaper and more expensive cards. Non-blended fees let merchants understand the price setting for different card types more accurately. Thus retailers know which cards are cheaper and potentially should be encouraged to use them via steering mechanisms (such as: default payment options, loyalty steering or price differentiation: rebates and surcharges).

Table 4 Merchant service charge (MSC) setting structures

	Blended fee	*2-component non-blended fee (IF+)*	*3-component non-blended fee (IF++)*
Merchant service charge (in %)	Single MSC on all cards	Interchange fee + other scheme and acquiring fees	Interchange fee + scheme fees + acquiring fee

Source Own compilation

1.2.2 *Rationale Behind Interchange Fees in Baxter's Model*

In his seminal paper, Baxter (1983) clarifies the rationale behind interchange fees. They address externalities that are characteristic for two-sided markets where choices depend on two actors: consumers and merchants. In the market for payment instruments every party weighs the costs and benefits of a payment method, e.g. cash and a payment card, and they are likely, in certain circumstances, to prefer a card payment. In Baxter's model, the issuer charges a transaction fee to the payment card consumer (f_c) while the acquirer charges a transaction fee to the merchant (f_m). Baxter's model assumes perfect competition between issuing and acquiring institutions, which implies they do not make profits (f_c equals the issuer's marginal costs denoted by c_i and f_m equals the acquirer's marginal costs denoted by c_a). Suppose that the consumer and the merchant value card payments and obtain a joint benefit that exceeds the joint costs of the issuer and the acquirer ($b_c + b_m > c_i + c_a$), but that the cost of a card transaction for the issuer is higher than a relative benefit of paying by card instead of cash for the consumer ($c_i > b_c$). In such a case, the consumer does not opt for payment by card although the merchant is willing to accept it over cash and collectively they would be better-off choosing card.

With an interchange fee paid by the acquirer to the issuer, this usage externality could be corrected and the socially optimal (card) transaction concluded. Without an interchange fee, the consumer would choose cash, thus exerting a negative externality on the merchant and they would not be able to extract the surplus as a two-sided actor. Note that in Baxter's model the interchange fee could go in the other way (from issuer to acquirer) if the merchant were more price sensitive than the consumer.

Baxter's model was grounded on simplified assumptions. Consumers and merchants were regarded as homogenous, and issuers and acquirers as perfectly competitive. The latter translated into a complete pass-through of the interchange fee back to consumers via lower issuer fees. In Baxter's model price differentiation between payment instruments, open to Coasian bargaining, was not possible; the "no-surcharge rule" held.

The theoretical literature on Baxter's model and the economics of interchange fees has been flourishing and many of the simplified and unrealistic assumptions have been relaxed. Selectively they are discussed below to provide a theoretical background for further investigation of interchange fee reforms. An extensive overview of the literature is made by Verdier (2011) and Rysman and Wright (2015). There are still many more theoretical than empirical studies but the number of the latter is also growing.

The socially optimum level of the Baxter interchange fee (if) assumes that the total merchant benefit less marginal acquirer costs ($if = b_m - c_a$) is transferred to the consumer. The Baxter interchange fee corresponds closely with the concept of a tourist test introduced by Rochet and Tirole (2007, 2011), which verifies merchant's indifference to the consumer's choice of a payment instrument (cash or card). The Baxter interchange fee maximises the welfare of consumers, in other words it maximises the user surplus (Rysman and Wright 2015: 329–330).

In day-to-day life, the interchange fee rate may diverge from the socially optimum level. *Inter alia*, it is difficult to defend the hypothesis that issuers and acquirers are perfectly competitive, so that they have no market power. In many markets, the platform, that is the issuing banks and other acquiring payment service providers in the card business, managed to operate on high margins (in practice the issuing activity used to be more profitable, see, e.g. European Commission 2006). The card pricing policy of issuers and acquirers, sometimes quite complex, was of much help in increasing profits.

Fees imposed on consumers and merchants are of mixed categories, not only transaction-based and variable, but also fixed. In addition, fees are charged with regard to many card services. Usually, cardholders never pay variable payment fees, only fixed fees, e.g. a monthly fee, but they can be charged with other card-related fees (e.g. fees for cash withdrawals, interest charges and other credit card fees or, interrelated or bundled with debit cards fees associated with holding a current account at a bank—see previous section). On the other hand, merchants pay a bundle of fees, e.g. a fixed fee for renting a payment accepting device, a variable merchant service charge, and possibly many other fees, like fees for payment terminal service, bill statements, chargeback, etc. Therefore, the privately set interchange fee rate can be determined by issuers and acquirers' overall price strategies. In fact, also scheme fees play a role here.

Another caveat pertains to merchants. Not only the supply side of the payment market can have a collective market power but so can merchants. First, in reality they are heterogeneous, i.e. large retail grocery store chains attribute a different benefit to card payments than, for example, small bazaar shops (benefits differ across sectors of economic activity too, e.g. hotels and restaurants against service providers, such as hairdressers, doctors, lawyers). Second, they may have enough market power not to let all the reductions of regulatory interchange fee caps pass on instantly to consumers, in particular when retailing is concentrated. The pass-through effect is also important when analysing how quickly acquirers respond to decreases in interchange fees and transfer savings from these decreases to merchants (this issue is investigated in detail in Chapter 3 "Empirical Investigation of the Polish Interchange Fee Reform Effects").

In the simple Baxter's model setup, one could think of a situation in which a fraction of the merchant benefit is transferred to the consumer through lower interchange fees (if $< b_m - c_a$). In such a case, consumers share their hypothetical user surplus (welfare) with merchants. Note that in theoretical models of interchange fees the relative benefit of cards over cash for consumers and merchants is somewhat vague. Leaving fees and rewards aside, the benefit consumers derive from cards is better convenience and higher security, while merchants' benefits stem from increased customer satisfaction (more payment instruments available), possibly higher turnover, less fraud, shorter queues. The Polish central bank enumerates and describes consumers and merchants' card payment benefits (NBP 2012: 11–12). Many of the benefits depend on the perception of consumers and merchants (e.g. Polasik et al. 2012). Habits and behavioural aspects play a key role here (see, e.g. Schuh and Stavins 2012; Wang et al. 2015; Harasim 2016). Perception sometimes differs from facts (e.g. perceived security and true level of fraud, perceived and actual speed of payment) and can be influenced by promotional activities of payment service providers and card organisations.

1.2.3 Optimal Interchange Fees

The theory of two-sided markets holds that card usage and card acceptance, and thus the possible welfare, depend on how consumers and merchants are charged. The role of interchange fees is to balance each side's benefits by maximising the indirect network effects between the two groups. Merchant internalisation of consumer surplus resulting in worse terms for merchants and better terms for consumers as well as asymmetry between two sides of the market, taking a variety of forms (e.g. a differentiated platform control over prices charged to each side or non-similar preferences of consumers and merchants towards various payment methods) drive apart socially and privately optimal interchange fees (Rysman and Wright 2015: 304–305).

Schmalensee (2002) and Wright (2004b) show that welfare-, profit- and volume-maximising interchange fees might not be the same, given different assumptions about demand-side characteristics, homo- and heterogeneity of consumers and merchants, or about asymmetry in the degree of competition between issuers and acquirers. Verdier summarises all cases and presents them in a concise manner (Verdier 2011: 279–284). She also indicates some issues not directly solved by the theoretical literature, such as: should profits of banks be taken into account in measuring social welfare, since these profits can be invested in innovation, in development of new payment methods and in improved security of payments (Verdier 2011: 277 and 285). This argument is often raised by issuing banks when they face accusations about extracting rents in high interchange fees. Banks argue that interchange fees let them cover costs of issuing and that the excess value goes back to clients in the form of innovative products and security improvements.

Baxter's model was further developed by many economists. A paper by Rochet and Tirole (2002) turned out particularly influential, affecting the position of competition authorities, including the European Commission. Subsequent works of both economists provided competition watchdogs with even better grounds for regulating interchange fees. Rochet and Tirole (2002) demonstrated that an interchange fee can be higher than socially optimal. Market power of issuers may lead to higher interchange fees and overprovision of card payments if cards are too expensive for merchants to accept but at the same time give them a competitive advantage over competing retailers. Later, this phenomenon started to be called "business stealing" or "must-take-card" (e.g. Vickers 2005).

The conclusions from the model of Rochet and Tirole (2002), in which merchants are homogenous in card acceptance benefit, depend critically on the existence of the "no-surcharge rule". The French economists argue that in the absence of the "no-surcharge rule" between merchants able to price differently for card and cash at no cost, the interchange fee has no impact on the level of payment card services and the welfare of end users.

The "must-take card" phenomenon is two-dimensional. Firstly, it relates to the initial decision of merchants about starting to accept cards. Secondly, it has much to do with whether merchants with a terminal already installed are more inclined to accept a cash or a card payment. The first dimension of the must-take card phenomenon has been empirically studied by Bounie et al. (2016) who used French data on merchants and modelled them with Heckman selection regression. Depending on the assumption as to who was qualified as a "card non-liker" and a "card-liker", it appeared that the "must-take card" phenomenon applied to 3.9–13.5% of the merchant population in France and the "wanna-take" effect for the bulk of merchants in France: 64.4–54.8%. The remaining part of merchants simply did not accept cards ("card non-likers" *sensu largo*).

Wright (2004b) enriched the analysis of Rochet and Tirole. Not only did he assume consumers as heterogeneous but he applied this to merchants, as well. However, in one version of his model, Wright confirmed what Rochet and Tirole found out, that if some merchants try to position themselves better *vis-a-vis* others, then they are prone to accept to pay more for cards in merchant fees, which results in overall higher interchange fees. In Wright's analysis, socially optimal interchange fees can deviate from privately optimal ones for two reasons. The first one is issuers partially passing through merchants' benefit back to consumers in rebates or bonuses. The second reason reflects the finding that consumers and merchants may not fully internalise each others' payment method benefits. But this asymmetry in inframarginal effects may make the socially optimal interchange fees lower but also higher than the profit maximising interchange fee. Therefore, Wright remains sceptical about regulating interchange fees and sees no good justification for any such intervention.

Platform competition can be a factor in determining an interchange fee. If no card system has monopoly power, users of each side of the market can "multi-home", that is connect to more than one payment platform. Usually, there is more than one card scheme on the market (Visa, Mastercard, Diners Club, other international schemes or domestic payment card schemes such as: BankAxept in Norway, Dankort in Denmark or Cartes Bancaires in France). Besides, there are other payment instruments available like cash or, e.g. mobile wallets based on the credit transfers. Capturing all the multi-homing options would be a challenging task, given different characteristics and behaviour of consumers and merchants. Nevertheless, building on the previous literature and considering various cases, Guthrie and Wright (2007) show that competition between platforms does not necessarily yield a socially optimal interchange fee compared to when there is a market with only one card platform servicing consumers and merchants. Hence, competition between card platforms can give rise to higher interchange fees in such circumstances, when merchants accept cards of different schemes to get more business and satisfy all cardholders' interests. This argument could be used by policymakers in justifying the decision to step in on the card payments market, but they usually use another argument finding market failure at the issuing side of the market. The European Commission observed that international card organisations competed in attracting issuing banks by offering them higher interchange fees (the so-called reverse competition). Unfortunately, this practice contributed to the disappearance of a few cost-efficient domestic card schemes in Austria, Finland, Ireland, the Netherlands or the UK (European Commission 2015b) which were less profitable to issuers. Wang's theoretical analysis demonstrates that in maturing card markets, where convenience of card payments increases, it is more likely for international card schemes to vertically control the system and raise interchange fees for the benefit of issuers (Wang 2010).

In general, there are two methods of determining a suitable benchmark for the optimum level of interchange fees (Börestam and Schmiedel 2011). Neither of them is flawless but the second one is better established in the theory of two-sided markets and entails less moral hazard in inflating cost items.

The first method is based on the supply side approach. Under this method, three cost categories are included in calculations. They are issuer's costs of: payment processing, payment guarantee and free funding. All three activities have value for card payers and merchants. Payment guarantee and free funding are costs of credit cards rather than debit cards for issuers. Free funding and other card-related services generate negligible marginal costs but give issuing banks the chance to obtain additional profits, not always directly linked to the payments activity (e.g. interest-based profit generated on the credit granted, when credit card holder defaults on debt payment).

The second method, which eventually replaced the supply side approach in finding a benchmark for interchange fee rates, is known as a tourist test (or a merchant indifference test or an avoided-cost test). The tourist test was introduced by Rochet and Tirole (2007, 2011) and its concept closely relates to the must-take cards situation in which merchants are compelled to accept cards in fear of losing customers to competition. In order to make a merchant indifferent to whether a non-repeat customer (tourist) pays with his (debit/credit) card or cash, accepting a card payment cannot be more expensive than accepting a cash payment. A (multilateral) interchange fee that passes the tourist test helps maximise consumers' and merchants' joint surplus (welfare). The benefit of a card payment in the tourist test is measured indirectly, that is by comparing (debit/credit) card costs to costs of the closest alternative payment instrument at the counter-cash.

In practical terms, variable costs are taken into account and fixed costs are omitted from calculations, because they do not affect merchant's decision about accepting a payment instrument at the counter. What affects this decision are marginal costs of an additional payment transaction. Most typically, studies devoted to calculating interchange fee rates compliant with the tourist test assume that variable costs of payment instrument change linearly. As a consequence, average variable costs equalise with marginal costs. One of the difficulties in calculations is to separate fixed costs of payment instruments from variable costs and to decide about the nature of variable costs (transaction-linked vs. sales-linked). The general formula for a tourist test conformant multilateral interchange fee (TT MIF) is:

$$\text{TT MIF}_{\text{two-part}} = \alpha_{\text{cash}} - \alpha_{\text{card}} + (\beta_{\text{cash}} - \beta_{\text{card}})x$$

where

α_{cash} and α_{card}—average variable cost per one additional cash/card transaction,

β_{cash} and β_{card}—average variable cost per one additional euro of cash/card sales,

x—value of transaction.

Figure 4 illustrates how to calculate the TT MIF and what the difference between the actual MIF and the TT MIF (or the MIT MIF: merchant indifference test compliant multilateral interchange fee) is.

TT MIFs change according to the transaction value. Frequently, studies compute TT MIFs for average card payment transaction values reflecting a static situation when one examines whether cards are not too costly in a given moment of time. In doing so, it is appropriate to benchmark to the amount of an average card payment. Including other transaction values, however, proves suitable for capturing market dynamics in substitution of payments instruments and anticipating likely decreases of an average card transaction value triggered by the contactless revolution.

The tourist test started to be used in the second half of the first decade of the twenty-first century. The European Commission adopted this methodology in antitrust actions against VISA and Mastercard

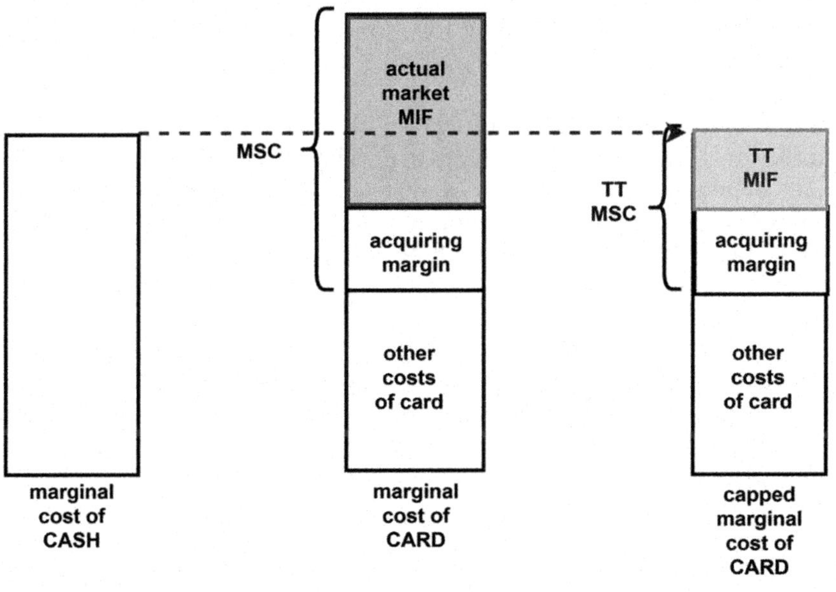

Fig. 4 Graphic illustration of the tourist test compliant multilateral interchange fee (TT MIF) (*Source* Janecskó A. [2015] *European Commission's Survey on Merchants' Costs of Processing Cash and Card Payments. Final Results*, presentation at III International Congress on Non-cash Payments, 18 March, Warsaw)

(cases: EC vs. MasterCard 2007; EC vs. Visa 2008). In 2015 the European Commission published a comprehensive analysis of merchants' costs leading to a determination of TT MIFs in the European Union, where it used data mainly from the survey of large merchants from ten biggest European countries. Empirical application of the tourist test in the economic literature was done by Górka for Poland (2012, 2013, 2014), Jonker and Plooij for the Netherlands (2013) and Layne-Farrar for the USA (2013).

In extenso, the issues connected with the tourist test application as well as the TT concept as such are analysed by Górka (2014). Simply put, every TT application relies on surveys of merchant costs of processing cash and card payments and requires recognising the nature of costs. It is not only compulsory to distinguish between fixed and variable (by number and by value) costs, but also between external and internal or between pecuniary and non-pecuniary (monetary and non-monetary) costs. To obtain robust results it helps to scrutinise cost items and conduct a scenario analysis of testing functions of cash and card costs under different conditions.

One common conclusion for all of the above studies is that the lower the transaction value, the lower the TT MIF. Below a certain transaction value, it becomes negative. The threshold amount is different depending on the study. Market characteristics play a role here. This conclusion implies that cash is a cost-efficient payment instrument in low-value transactions, something unambiguously found also by numerous studies of social (resource) costs performed by central banks (e.g. Schmiedel et al. 2012).

Layne-Farrar's (2013) for the US market took account of merchant's heterogeneity. She calculated TT MIFs for merchants of different types (e.g. restaurants, gas stations, supermarkets, convenience stores) and of different sizes, and checked whether a TT MIF is above or below the regulatory interchange fee cap brought in by the Durbin Amendment (DA) in October 2010. When comparing cash and cards for average retailers and for most of the merchant types (except for large supermarkets), the TT MIF was either below a DA MIF cap or about right. It did not hold true when comparing cards and cheques. In this pair of payment instruments, DA MIF cap benchmarking to the TT MIF appeared to be too high.

The calculations of Górka (2014) and of the European Commission (2015a) produced similar results and provided a solid backing for regulations capping interchange fees in Poland and in the EU at the level of 0.2 and 0.3% (for debit and credit cards respectively). Both studies were much alike in methodology and approach, while differing on a number of issues, such as, for instance, the coverage of retail sections of the economic activity or the merchant size (for more detailed comparison of both studies see Górka 2014). The European study covered as much as 12.4% of all card transactions in the whole EU 28 but the cost data were taken from large merchant survey. In contrast, the Polish study concentrated on small retailers. There are differences among small and large merchants. For example, smaller merchants have less bargaining power against acquirers, hence their MSCs comprise higher acquiring fees. In both studies, the robustness of TT MIF application was verified by using a scenario approach consisting in changing the composition of fixed and variable costs. Extending the time horizon or including more fixed costs into calculations deteriorates the position of cash, and sets TT MIFs higher. On the aggregated level, for the homogenous average merchant and for the average card transaction value:

- The Polish study showed that a TT MIF of a card (debit and credit combined) should be set at −0.16 to 0.18% depending on the scenario.
- The EC study showed that in a short-and medium-term horizon a TT MIF ranges from −0.07 to 0.16% for debit cards and −0.21 to 0.13% for credit cards and in the long-term horizon debit and credit card TT MIFs are between 0.19 and 0.47%.

Jonker and Plooij (2013) estimated the TT MIF for Dutch data from 2002 and 2009 and obtained results and conclusions in line with those from the Polish and the EC study. According to their calculations, a TT MIF rose from 0.2 to 0.5% because of negative scale effects of cash and positive scale effects, and technological improvements (like faster transaction processing at the shop counter) in debit cards. Having in mind a declining share of cash in retail purchases and an increasing role of debit cards in European societies, Dutch authors in the extension of their paper (Bolt et al. 2013) expressed the view that tourist test may well turn out to be a tourist trap, justifying higher MIFs.

On the other hand, an application of this method of determining a benchmark for interchange fees may evolve. There is an increasing number of new methods of non-cash payments available at points of sale.

The online (internet or in-app remote payments) and the offline (POS payments) worlds converge. Mobile wallets and mobile payments are gaining popularity. In mobile payment systems (e.g. MobilePay in Denmark, Blik in Poland) the underlying payment method is not always card payment; it can also be a simple credit transfer. The second Payment Services Directive going live in 2018 further fuels development of new forms of payment based on the credit transfers, because it enables payment initiation services. With a growing acceptance base for alternative non-cash payment methods, they can start serving as a TT MIF benchmark for cards of international card schemes.

1.2.4 Scheme Business Rules ("No-Surcharge", "Honour-All-Cards") and the Blending Practice

The success of four-party card systems lies in mass adoption. Scheme business rules, such as "no-surcharge" (NSR, called also "non-discrimination rule") or "honour-all-cards" (HACR) help reducing cardholder inconvenience, but at the same time they may affect competition between payment instruments and contribute to higher prices of goods or to maintaining excessive interchange fees. Card surcharging takes place when merchants impose a higher price on customers paying by card than by cash. Honour-all-cards rule obliges retailers to accept all card types within a given card scheme, regardless of their MSCs. The blending practice prevents merchants from distinguishing between more expensive and cheaper cards and gives them no information about the MSC structure, unlike the IF+or IF++ setting (see Sect. 1.2.1 "Interchange Fee and Other Fees in Four-Party Card System"). The blending practice is popular among small merchants for its simplicity, and may even be considered attractive to them.

In payments, market failure may arise from the negative externality exerted on non-card customers (non-platform users) who face the same price when paying by card and in cash, i.e. when there is price coherence (Tirole 2015). The NSR allows card payment networks to "tax" cash users. With no possibility for merchants to signal the price of cards to consumers there is a risk of rising or petrifying an excessive interchange fee and MSC on the market. According to Tirole (2015) this problem does not exist when the MSC (and so the interchange fee) follows the Pigovian principle or, in other words, finds itself at the tourist test compliant level. Alternatively, differentiating the price by surcharging a card transaction has the same effect as discounting a cash transaction, provided it is done by an amount that equalises the marginal costs and benefits of two instruments. Zenger (2011) demonstrates that this "perfect surcharging" by merchants and interchange fees that satisfy TT are allocatively equivalent. *Ergo*, both methods are interchangeable and facilitate removal of the potential market failure inherent in four-corner card payment networks.

Surcharging functions as a safety valve. Constraints on NSR may lead to the over-usage of cards and too high prices for cash users, not desirable from the perspective of the social planner. Schwartz and Vincent (2006) argue, based on the model assuming merchants to be local monopolies and payment methods to be exogenous to each other, that NSR increases issuers' profits. NSR can do harm even to card users, in absence of reward programmes, i.e. if issuers do not transfer any fraction of high interchange fees back to cardholders. On the other hand, reward programmes can give rise to higher interchange and merchant fees. Although card users' welfare is undiminished, cash users sustain a loss (Schwartz and Vincent 2006). Pretty consistent conclusions are drawn by Saxén (2014). NSR causes prices to rise not only for merchants accepting cards but for all merchants. NSR contributes to less competition in the merchants' market and may result in socially excessive card use. However, the right to surcharge for imperfectly competitive merchants can also translate into socially too little card use (Saxén 2014). Also, another drawback of lifting NSR can be excessive surcharging when merchants use the opportunity of price add-ons to make profit (see the case of Australia in Chapter 2). Whether surcharging merchants reduce their prices for cash users is a matter for empirical investigation.

Widespread surcharging (equal to acceptance costs) would render interchange fees neutral or irrelevant. In practice, however, surcharging is not popular with merchants even if they are allowed to use it. There is explanation for that. Putting surcharging in action entails management costs to merchants, especially in a non-blended surcharge setting, that is different surcharges for different types of cards (high costs of calculating, organising, displaying surcharges in a transparent way to customers prior to payment). Moreover, merchants may be afraid of losing customers if they surcharge them (business-stealing effect).

Price differentiation can take either a form of a surcharge or a discount. The former steering practice discourages consumers more from selecting a card. Stavins and Shy (2015) find from the 2012 consumer diary survey in the US that none of the pricing differentiation strategies by merchants was frequently exploited. Cash or debit card discounts were slightly more popular than credit card surcharges, but on average US merchants took advantage of discounting or surcharging for not more than 1.2–1.8% transactions. Nevertheless, for specific merchant categories, such as: gas stations and auto repair these practices enjoy more popularity because there they are accepted as a norm in the USA. 8.7 and 5.7% gas station transactions were subject to cash discounting and credit card surcharging, respectively (Stavins and Shy 2015).

In the European Union, the first Payment Services Directive (2007) entitled merchants to use both rebating and surcharging but member states were able to go for a national option to prohibit or limit the right to surcharge itself. 14 EU countries did so, while 12 allowed surcharging. One country (Denmark) prohibited surcharging on debit cards but let credit cards be surcharged (European Commission 2013: 131–132). The 2011 Consumer Right Directive banned surcharging that would exceed the costs incurred by merchants. The level of surcharge amounted on average to 2–3% of the price. Compared to the United States, more merchants in Europe took advantage of the right to surcharge, based on the merchants' survey commissioned by the European Commission for the purpose of assessing the impact of payments legislation (Table 5). Among countries that allowed surcharging, merchants used it mainly for credit cards and in particular sectors, such as hotels and hospitality, catering and restaurants, entertainment and recreation.

Table 5 Presence of surcharging on credit cards in selected EU countries

Country	*Non-surcharging merchants (%)*	*Surcharging merchants (%)*
Belgium	93	7
Denmark	91	9
Finland	99	1
France[a]	96	4
Germany	91	9
Ireland	86	14
Netherlands	90	10
Spain	92	8
UK	86	14

[a]In France the law did not allow for surcharging but nonetheless surcharging was present
Source European Commission (2013), ***Commission Staff Working Document (Impact assessment for PSD2 and IF Regulation)***, SWD (2013) 288, p. 132

The Interchange Fee Regulation in Europe upheld the right to use the full spectrum of pricing steering practices by merchants, however, the revised Payment Services Directive (PSD2) coming effectively into force in January 2018 banned surcharging for regulated cards with capped interchange fees.

Surcharging can have a positive impact on card payment acceptance. Such is the conclusion from Jonker's empirical study of Dutch merchants (2011). Surcharging makes merchants less reluctant to accept cards and strengthens their negotiating power with acquirers. If surcharges are added to more expensive credit cards then more socially efficient debit cards may benefit. Competition between merchants is another important factor. Merchants, which are local monopolies, tend to surcharge more likely than merchants facing moderate or fierce competition (Jonker 2011).

One of the barriers to surcharging originates from the HACR and blending. Merchants cannot consider surcharging an option when they are charged a blended MSC and forced to accept all cards within a brand. In the theoretical model of Rochet and Tirole (2008), tying of more expensive and cheaper cards raises social welfare due to a rebalancing effect even if interchange fees for protected expensive cards remain too high. The model tests different assumptions, such as: substitutability between the two cards, platform differentiation and merchant heterogeneity. Direct benefits derived from the HACR for card payers are clear. They never have to fear a situation where they enter a shop and their card is not accepted. The flip side of the coin is that the usage of more socially efficient debit cards can be not sufficiently incentivised, because credit cards are treated at par with debit cards. HACR and blending demonstrate there is little economic sense for merchants to make any effort to make costs of different means of payment transparent and to steer customers to any choice of a payment instrument.

Note that the abolition of the HACR has been enforced by legal actions on different continents in the world (e.g. the EU, USA, Australia) but it was applied to honour-all-products rule and not to honour-all-issuers rule. The latter could possibly lead to a discrimination of particular banks and cardholders.

The European Commission estimated, in a conservative scenario simulation based on 2011 data from the ECB, that the removal of HACR could result in a 5% shift between debit and credit cards in the European Union corresponding to EUR 370 million savings for merchants yearly if interchange fees would have stayed unregulated and EUR 95 million for cards under 0.2/0.3% interchange fee caps (European Commission 2013: 213).

The counterproductive effect of blending exists especially when there are high discrepancies between interchange fees attributed to different types of cards. Nevertheless, charging merchants a uniform MSC is always anti-competitive. Blending is not a sheer scheme rule, as it is imposed on merchants by acquirers. In principle, it gives more benefit to credit cards, which are typically subject to higher MIFs.

In Mastercard and Visa payment networks, credit card usage, due to higher interchange fees and other sources of income, tend to be more incentivised by issuing banks which offer reward programmes to cardholders. Arango et al. (2015) empirical study of the Canadian market brings corroborating evidence that both cash and debit card payments suffer from credit card reward programmes. When they are in place, the likelihood of paying with a credit card rises by a range of 3.6–12.8 percentage points for transactions of 25 USD and above.

1.2.5 Framework for Assessing the Impact of Interchange Fee Regulation

Competition authorities initiate antitrust proceedings against card schemes on formal grounds. Frequently, the method of multilateral interchange fee setting has been considered to be a collective practice restricting competition (e.g. in Spain or Poland). Several economists argue that the method itself is not anti-competitive, it may even be more efficient than bilateral negotiations (see, e.g. Chang and Evans 2000). However, the problem arises when interchange fees are socially too high or the market fails in another way, resulting in a fee structure that does not maximise shared welfare of consumers and merchants. There are proponents and opponents of regulating interchange fees. In favour of regulation are e.g.: Frankel (1998) or Vickers (2005), while others call for refraining from any direct intervention in the card payments market, e.g. Rysman (2007) or Wright (2004b). Börestam and Schmiedel (2011) refer to the regulation as *ultima ratio* but implicitly suggest that it is possible for card schemes to operate even without interchange fees. They give examples of national card schemes from Denmark, Finland, Luxembourg and the Netherlands operating without interchange fees. Leinonen (2011) is even more definite by stating that, undoubtedly, decreasing interchange fees to zero would be the best solution in that it would boost competition between payment methods and deprive issuers of a possibility to take profit from acquirers. However, unlike, e.g. Tirole, Leinonen argues that it is not card users who cross-subsidise cash users but the opposite holds true instead. Therefore, eliminating interchange fees would benefit cards.

This section presents a framework for evaluating benefits and costs (or positives and negatives) of regulatory interventions capping MIFs and eliminating practices considered harmful for the payments market. In general, there are a few areas to be taken into account, plainly visible from the links between parties in the four-corner model setup. Assessing interchange fee reforms requires examining the impact on all major stakeholders: consumers, merchants, acquirers, issuers and payment organisations. The conceptual framework consists of three areas. They refer to the transmission mechanism of interchange fee reductions between parties and to the effects associated with the reduction.

- Area 1, transmission channel: acquirer → merchant → consumer (cardholder)
- Area 2, transmission channel: issuer → consumer (cardholder)
- Area 3, card scheme domain: payment organisation—issuer—acquirer

Area 1

The pass-through rate of the reduction in MIFs determines how quickly effects can be visible for the merchant side and subsequently to consumers. Effectiveness of transferring the benefits of lower interchange fees in the acquirer → merchant → consumer transmission channel depends on the competition in the acquiring market and in the merchant market (and its segments), and on the asymmetry of information. Typically, merchants and consumers are less informed than payment service providers. Until merchants become aware of the decrease in MIFs, acquirers have the possibility to keep higher margins. The composition of the MSC temporarily changes to the advantage of acquirers. Obviously, they can only earn more from those merchants which are charged a blended MSC, because the pass-through of interchange fee changes for merchants with MSCs in the IF+ or IF++ setting occurs instantly as soon as the MIF reduction becomes effective. On the other hand, the competition for new merchants should start immediately after or even before the reduction.

There are two aspects to be verified, one corresponding to the network effect and the other one, to the fees for merchants and prices for consumers.

Claim 1
lower interchange fees→ lower merchant fees→ higher growth of card payments acceptance network (new merchants)

Claim 2
broader card acceptance network→ stronger indirect network effect→ higher utility of cards for cardholders and merchants→ higher card usage

Claims 1 and 2 are anchored directly to the two-sided markets theory, which stresses the need to increase indirect network effects between two groups of entities. If interchange and merchant transaction fees are set too high, then card acceptance network may not grow fast enough. Decreasing IFs can positively make it develop more quickly and contribute to higher utility of cards for consumers and merchants. Next, additional card payments can be triggered not only at new merchants but also at merchants which have long accepted cards. The bandwagon starts rolling and the card usage rises. Looking in a broader context, it can have consequences for the choice of payment instruments. Card payments featuring stronger network effect may replace cash payments faster.

Claim 3
lower interchange fees→ lower merchant fees→ lower prices for consumers

Claim 3 assumes that as interchange fees fall, the competition within the acquiring market rises. Primarily, acquirers start attracting new merchants for which costs of card acceptance have been too high until now. In addition, the level of churn increases, since acquirers attract merchants with fees lower than those of competitors. Merchants become better positioned in terms of their bargaining power against acquirers. The larger the merchant, i.e. the higher card payments volume it generates, the better its negotiating power. Merchant fees fall. Merchants experience lower costs of card acceptance. Then, depending on the degree of competition within the merchant market (a reaction in different merchant sectors may be different, e.g. in retail trade vs. in hotels and restaurants), consumers may benefit directly from lower prices of goods and services. Alternatively, as merchant fees are only one of many price components and of relatively little significance compared to others, the competition can result in slower growth of prices.

Note that in all causal mechanisms demonstrated by claims 1, 2 and 3 there is ample room for research on assessing effects of abolishing scheme business rules (NSR or HACR) or of other transparency measures. They affect actors in the acquirer→ merchant→ consumer transmission channel.

Area 2

Facing fall in interchange fee revenues, issuing banks may feel tempted to raise cardholder fees. Consistent with the theory of two-sided markets is the following:

Claim 4

lower interchange fees→ lower interchange fee revenues for issuers→ higher cardholder fees (or other card-related fees, e.g. accountholder fees).

Claim 4 identifies what is occurring between issuing banks and their clients—cardholders or, more narrowly speaking, consumers holding their debit and credit cards. All debit card holders must keep a current account at the bank (it can possibly change after payment service providers in Europe will have utilised new provisions of the revised Payment Services Directive on payment initiation services and account information services). Credit card holders are not compelled to have a current account at the issuing bank but they often do. Issuers may attempt to pass the interchange fee reduction on to cardholders by raising cardholder fees and by decreasing rewards in loyalty programmes, thus recouping lost income. The pricing strategy of banks may be more complex than just increasing periodic card fees. They may increase other fees, for instance for cash withdrawals or for holding a payment account, or increase penalty charges on credit cards. The competition within the issuing sector is a countervailing factor.

Gains from decreasing interchange fees for consumers holding cards and for merchants are twofold. *Ceteris paribus*, assuming that, for example, neither innovation nor security of payments suffer, the demand side of the payments market (that is cardholders and merchants combined) experience a welfare increase through two types of savings. One in the form of realised financial gains from lower interchange fees, two in the form of alternative financial gains coming from future savings calculated by comparing actual interchange fee revenues of banks with hypothetical interchange fee revenues of banks assuming that IF rates would stay unchanged at the level from before the reduction. Financial (actual and opportunity) gains may be of lesser magnitude due to the pass-through effect described by claim 4.

Area 3

A card scheme domain can also undergo changes following interchange fee reductions. Unlike previous causal mechanisms shown above, what may occur in the scheme domain is barely analysed in the theoretical economic literature. Furthermore, there may be some practical difficulty in tracking all, sometimes subtle, modifications of scheme fees and scheme rules presented to issuers and acquirers.

One potential risk is that card schemes may be willing to compensate for decreased interchange fee revenues to issuers by reducing issuer fees and introducing a kind of rebalancing mechanism through scheme fees charged in higher proportions to acquirers. That would mean circumventing the interchange fee reform. On the other hand, payment organisations may treat the interchange fee regulation in a neutral way, because it does not affect their business directly. Card organisations can hardly oppose legally lifted scheme business rules such as NSR or HACR.

Claim 5

lower interchange fees (and possibly abolished NSR and HACR)→ no or minor changes to the aggregate level of scheme fees→ more incentives for issuers and acquirers to develop more cost-efficient new payment instruments→ more innovation and competition on the payments market

When interchange fees go down, it is hardly likely that scheme fees will fall. They will typically remain pretty much the same, given payment organisations' limited sensitivity to interchange fee decreases. However, for issuers the situation changes diametrically. Even if they were not fond of the scheme fee level before the interchange fee reduction, they become more sensitive afterwards when a great part of their already diminished card issuing revenues flows to payment organisations cutting card profits. As an outcome, market conditions change in favour of payment instruments with lower processing and other internal fees. Banks and non-bank payment service providers become more willing to support or develop innovative and more cost-efficient payment instruments in a more transparent business model. In addition, elimination of NSR and HACR weakens the position of cards compared to cash and other cashless means of payments. The overall competition of the payment market improves.

The presented framework for analysing impacts of interchange fee regulatory decreases encompasses three areas for assessment, which are specific to parties from the four-corner model. Claims formulated in each of the areas are established in the literature and in policymakers' approach. Whether they hold true needs to be tested empirically and discussed on real-life cases. The next two chapters discuss interchange fee reforms in European countries (with special emphasis on Poland and Spain), Australia and the USA.

Bibliography

Arango C., Huynh K., Sabetti L. (2015) *Consumer Payment Choice: Merchant Card Acceptance Versus Pricing Incentives*, "Journal of Banking and Finance", No. 55 (June), pp. 130–141.

Armstrong M. (2006) *Competition in Two Sided Markets*. "The RAND Journal of Economics", Vol. 37, No. 3, pp. 668–691.

Arthur B. (1999) *Competing Technologies, Increasing Returns, and Lock-In by Historical Events*, "The Economic Journal", Vol. 99, No. 394 (March), pp. 116–131.

Baxter W. (1983) *Bank Interchange of Transactional Paper, Legal and Economic Perspectives*, "Journal of Law and Economics", Vol. 26, No. 3 (October), pp. 541–588.

Belleflamme P., Toulemonde E. (2016) *Who Benefits from Increased Competition Among Sellers on B2C Platforms?* "Research in Economics", Vol. 70, No. 4, pp. 741–751.

Bolt W., Jonker N., Plooij M. (2013) *Tourist Test or Tourist Trap? Unintended Consequences of Debit Card Interchange Fee Regulation*, DNB Working Paper 405.

Börestam A., Schmiedel H. (2011) *Interchange Fees in Card Payments*, ECB Occasional Paper Series No. 131.

Bounie D., Francois A., Van Hove L. (2016) *Merchant Acceptance of Payment Cards: "Must Take" or "Wanna Take"?* "Review of Network Economics", Vol. 15, No. 3, pp. 117–146.

Caillaud B., Jullien B. (2003) *Chicken-and-Egg: Competition Among Intermediation Service Providers*, "The RAND Journal of Economics", Vol. 34, No. 2, pp. 309–328.

Chang H., Evans D. (2000) *The Competitive Effects of the Collective Setting of Interchange Fees by Payment Card System*, "The Antitrust Bulletin", No. 641.

Choi J. (2010) *Tying in Two-Sided Markets with Multi-homing*, "The Journal of Industrial Economics", Vol. 58, No. 3, pp. 607–626.

Doganoglu T., Wright J. (2006) *Multihoming and Compatibility*, "International Journal of Industrial Organization", Vol. 24, No. 1, pp. 45–67.

European Commission (2006) *Interim Report I Payments Cards*, Commission DG Document, Sectoral Inquiry, Brussels, 12 April.

European Commission (EC) (2007) *Case COMP/M.4523 Travelport/Worldspan, Commission Decision C(2007) 3938 of 21 August 2007.*

European Commission (2013) *Commission Staff Working Document (Impact assessment for PSD2 and IF Regulation)*, SWD (2013) 288.

European Commission (2015a) *Survey on Merchants' Costs of Processing Cash Payments: Final Results*, Report, March, Brussel.

European Commission (2015b) *The Interchange Fees Regulation* in "Competition Policy brief" Occasional Discussion Papers by the Competition Directorate–General of the European Commission, No. 3, June 2015.

Evans D. (2003) *The Antitrust Economics of Multi-sided Platform Markets*, "Yale Journal on Regulation" Vol. 20, No. 2, pp. 325–381.

Evans D., Noel M. (2008) *The Analysis of Mergers That Involve Multisided Platform Businesses*, "Journal of Competition Law and Economics", Vol. 4, No. 3, pp. 663–695.

Evans D., Schmalensee R. (2005) *The Industrial Organization of Markets with Two-Sided Platforms*, Working Paper National Bureau of Economic Research, Cambridge, Published (2007) in "Competition Policy International", Vol. 3, No. 1 (Spring), pp. 150–179.

Evans D., Chang H., Joyce S. (2013) *The Impact of the U.S. Debit Card Interchange Fee Regulation on Consumer Welfare: An Event Study Analysis*, University of Chicago Coase-Sandor Institute for Law & Economics Research Paper No. 658.

Filistrucchi L., Geradin D., van Damme E., Affeldt P. (2014) *Market Definition in Two-Sided Markets: Theory and Practice*, "Journal of Competition Law and Economics", Vol. 10, No. 2 (June), pp. 293–339.

Frankel A. (1998) *Monopoly and Competition in the Supply and Exchange of Money*, "Antitrust Law Journal", No. 66, pp. 331–361.

Górka J. (2009) *Konkurencyjność form pieniądza i instrumentów płatniczych* (title in English: *Competitiveness of Money Forms and Payment Instruments*), CeDeWu.

Górka J. (2012) *Badanie kosztów akceptacji gotówki i kart płatniczych wśród polskich przedsiębiorców* (title in English: *Study of Cash and Cards Payment*

Acceptance Costs Among Polish Merchants), Report in the Research Project of FROB, NBP and FoM UW.

Górka J. (2013) *Efektywność instrumentów płatniczych w Polsce* (title in English: *Efficiency of Payment Instruments in Poland*), Publishing House of the Faculty of Management, University of Warsaw.

Górka J. (2014) *Merchant Indifference Test Application—A Case for Revising Interchange Fee Level in Poland*, in "The Usage, Costs and Benefits of Cash—Revisited: Proceedings of the 2014 International Cash Conference", Deutsche Bundesbank, pp. 75–151.

Guthrie G., Wright J. (2007) *Competing Payment Schemes*, "Journal of Industrial Economics", Vol. 55, No. 1, pp. 37–67.

Hagiu A., Hałaburda H. (2014) *Information and Two-Sided Platform Profits*, "International Journal of Industrial Organization", Vol. 34, No. 1, pp. 25–35.

Hagiu A., Jullien B. (2014) *Search Diversion and Platform Competition*, "International Journal of Industrial Organization", Vol. 33, No. 1, pp. 48–60.

Harasim J. (2016) *The Shift from Cash to Non-cash Transactions*, In Górka J. (ed.) "Transforming Payment Systems in Europe", Palgrave Macmillan, pp. 28–69.

Janecskó A. (2015) *European Commission's Survey on Merchants' Costs of Processing Cash and Card Payments: Final Results*, Presentation at III International Congress on Non-cash Payments, 18 March, Warsaw.

Jonker N. (2011) *Card Acceptance and Surcharging: The Role of Costs and Competition*, DNB Working Papers 300.

Jonker N., Plooij M. (2013) *Tourist Test Interchange Fees for Card Payments: Down or Out?*, "Journal of Financial Market Infrastructures", Vol. 1, No. 4, pp. 51–72.

Katz M., Shapiro C. (1985) *Network Externalities, Competition, and Compatibility*, "The American Economic Review", Vol. 75, No. 3 (June), pp. 424–440.

Layne-Farrar A. (2013) *Assessing the Durbin Amendment's Debit Card Interchange Fee Cap: An Application of the "Tourist Test" to US Retailer Data*, "Review of Network Economics", Vol. 12, No. 2, pp. 157–182.

Leinonen H. (2011) *Debit Card Interchange Fees Generally Lead to Cash-Promoting Cross-Subsidisation*, Bank of Finland Research Discussion Papers No. 3.

Liebowitz S., Margolis S. (1995) *Path Dependence, Lock-In and History*, "Journal of Law, Economics and Organization", Vol. 11, No. 1, pp. 205–226.

Narodowy Bank Polski (NBP) (2012) *Analysis of the Functioning of the Interchange Fee in Cashless Transactions on the Polish Market*, NBP Report, Warsaw.

Payment Services Directive (EU) 2015/2366 of the European Parliament and of the Council of 25 November 2015 on Payment Services in the Internal Market (PSD2), OJ EU L 337/35.

Polasik M., Marzec J., Fiszeder P., Górka J. (2012) *Modelowanie wykorzystania metod płatności detalicznych na rynku polskim* (title in English: *Modelling of Retail Payment Methods Usage in Poland*), Working Papers of the National Bank of Poland, No. 265.

Rochet J., Tirole J. (2002) *Cooperation Among Competitors: Some Economics of Payment Card Associations*, "The RAND Journal of Economics", Vol. 33, No. 4, pp. 549–570.

Rochet J., Tirole J. (2003) *Platform Competition in Two-Sided Markets*, "Journal of the European Economic Association", Vol. 1, No. 4, pp. 990–1029.

Rochet J., Tirole J. (2006) *Two-Sided Markets: A Progress Report*, "The RAND Journal of Economics", Vol. 3, No. 3, pp. 645–667.

Rochet J., Tirole J. (2007) *Must-Take Cards and the Tourist Test*, DNB Working Papers 127.

Rochet J., Tirole J. (2008) *Tying in Two-Sided Markets and the Honor All Cards Rule*, "International Journal of Industrial Organization", Vol. 26, No. 6, pp. 1333–1347.

Rochet J., Tirole J. (2011) *Must-Take Cards: Merchant Discounts and Avoided Costs*, "Journal of the European Economic Association", Vol. 9, No. 3, pp. 462–495.

Rysman M. (2007) *An Empirical Analysis of Payment Card Usage*, "Journal of Industrial Economics", Vol. 55, No. 1, pp. 1–36.

Rysman M. (2009) *The Economics of Two-Sided Markets What Defines a Two-Sided Market?* "Journal of Economic Perspectives", Vol. 23, No. 3 (Summer), pp. 125–143.

Rysman M., Wright J. (2015) *The Economics of Payment Cards*, "Review of Network Economics", Vol. 13, No. 3, pp. 303–353.

Saxén F. (2014) *The No Surcharge Rule and Merchant Competition*, "Journal of Industry, Competition and Trade", Vol. 14, No. 1, pp. 39–66.

Schmalensee R. (2002) *Payment Systems and Interchange Fees*, "The Journal of Industrial Economics", Vol. 50, No. 2, pp. 103–122.

Schmiedel H., Kostova G., Ruttenberg W. (2012) *The Social and Private Costs of Retail Payment Instruments: A European Perspective*, ECB Occasional Paper Series No. 137.

Schuh S., Stavins J. (2012) *How Consumers Pay: Adoption and Use of Payments*, "Accounting and Finance Research", Vol. 2, No. 2, pp. 1–21.

Schwartz M., Vincent D. (2006) *The No Surcharge Rule and Card User Rebates: Vertical Control by a Payment Network*, "Review of Network Economics", Vol. 5, No. 1, pp. 72–102.

Stavins J., Shy O. (2015) *Journal of Behavioral and Experimental Economics Merchant Steering of Consumer Payment Choice: Evidence from a 2012 Diary Survey*, "Journal of Behavioral and Experimental Economics", Vol. 55, pp. 1–9.

Strauss M. (2017) *MasterCard Canada Sets New Tone in Fee Battle*, "The Globe and Mail", 16 February.

Tilburg Law and Economics Center (TILEC) at Tilburg University (2010) *Mergers in Two-Sided Markets—A Report to the NMa Tilburg Howrey LLP*, Report, June.

Tirole J. (2014) *Market Failures and Public Policy, Noble Prize Lecture*, December 8, Stockholm.

Tirole J. (2015) *Market Failures and Public Policy*, "American Economic Review", Vol. 105, No. 6, pp. 1665–1682.

Van Hove L. (1999) *Electronic Money and the Network Externalities Theory: Lessons for Real Life*, "Netnomics", Vol. 1, No. 2, pp. 137–171.

Verdier M. (2011) *Interchange Fees in Payment Card Systems: A Survey of the Literature* "Journal of Economic Surveys", Vol. 25, No. 2, pp. 273–297.

Vickers J. (2005) *Public Policy and the Invisible Price: Competition Law, Regulation and the Interchange Fee*, Proceedings—Payments System Research Conferences, Issue May, pp. 231–247.

Wang Z. (2010) *Market Structure and Payment Card Pricing: What Drives the Interchange?* "International Journal of Industrial Organization", Vol. 28, No. 1, pp. 86–98.

Wang R., Malthouse E., Krishnamurthi L. (2015) *On the Go: How Mobile Shopping Affects Customer Purchase Behavior*, "Journal of Retailing", Vol. 91, No. 2, pp. 217–234.

Williamson O. (2010) *Transaction Cost Economics: The Natural Progression*, "American Economic Review", Vol. 100, No. 2, pp. 673–690.

Wright J. (2004a) *One-sided Logic in Two-Sided Markets*, "Review of Network Economics", Vol. 3, No. 1, pp. 44–64.

Wright J. (2004b) *The Determinants of Optimal Interchange Fees in Payment Systems*, "Journal of Industrial Economics", Vol. 52, No. 1, pp. 1–26.

Zenger H. (2011) *Perfect Surcharging and the Tourist Test Interchange Fee*, "Journal of Banking and Finance", Vol. 35, No. 10, pp. 2544–2546.

CHAPTER 2

Interchange Fee Reforms in Various Countries

This chapter offers a global overview of card payment reforms in various countries. It starts with looking at public authorities' actions in the area of card payments. Public authorities' main objective is to cap interchange fees and, more seldom, merchant service charges. The actions cover also other issues with the aim to increase market transparency and limit market power of card networks and banks. Section 2.1 looks into the cases of public authorities' involvement in France, EU (competition cases), Mexico, Canada, Israel, India and China. In Sect. 2.2 three country cases—Australia, USA and Spain—are studied in detail according to the framework for assessing the impact of interchange fee reforms from Chapter 1. Each of the five claims from three areas, with regard to transmission channels of interchange fee reductions, is tested for every country. Then, all three country cases are summarised in one table and their impact is assessed according to multiple criteria (impact of transparency measures, impact on: merchant service charges, card acceptance, card usage, prices, bank revenues and cardholder charges, four-party card schemes, competition and innovation and, eventually, the overall impact). Good and bad sides of the reforms are presented. Section 2.3 deals with the most recent and complex European Union's Interchange Fee Regulation. Its discussion includes its timetable, scope, caps, separation of scheme and processing as well as business and transparency rules. Practical problems with some provisions of the EU Regulation, the process of their implementation and the importance for card schemes

J. Górka, *Interchange Fee Economics*,
https://doi.org/10.1007/978-3-030-03041-4_2

and other parties are also analysed. Finally, this section refers to the Regulation's review clause, i.e. the upcoming European Commission's impact assessment of the Regulation planned for mid-2019.

2.1 Global Outlook on Public Authorities' Involvement in Card Payments

The interchange fees and scheme practices such as NSR or HACR have been on the radar of competition authorities for a long time. In general, competition watchdogs file investigations against global card networks: Visa and Mastercard, but sometimes also other schemes are subject to antitrust proceedings.

In 2011 the French competition office expressed its concerns about interbank fees being jointly set by 130 banks from the *Groupement des Cartes Bancaires*. The French national four-party card scheme is a major player in France for domestic card payments, outranking by far Visa and Mastercard. French banks were at risk of severe fines unless they could prove that they satisfy the conditions laid down in Article 101(3) of the Treaty on the Functioning of the European Union (TFEU hereafter), i.e. that their agreement on the level of fees contributes to a more efficient production or distribution of goods or to promoting technical and economic progress, with consumers obtaining a fair share of the benefit. The French competition office used the tourist test and also measured issuer card costs (see Sect. 1.2.3 "Optimal Interchange Fees"). In the course of the proceedings, French banks committed to reduce the fee by 36%, from 0.47 to 0.30% on average, which was accepted by the competition office and put an end to the issue (ECN 2012: 34). After the decrease in interchange fees in the domestic Carte Bancaire system, the French competition office looked into other card schemes, including Visa and Mastercard. In 2013 international card networks agreed to lower their interchange fees for domestic payments and set the average fee rate at 0.28% (Hayashi and Maniff 2017).

In 2012 the European Competition Network (ECN 2012), consisting of national competition authorities in the European Union and the Competition Directorate General of the European Commission, prepared an information paper on competition enforcement in the payments sector. The ECN report covered 22 European countries and the pan-European level (cases initiated by the European Commission). It turned out that an overwhelming majority of cases were related to card payments and interchange fees. Formally antitrust proceedings were opened based on Article 101 of the TFEU prohibiting all agreements between undertakings, decisions by associations of undertakings and concerted practices that restrict competition (Mastercard after going public in 2006 and undergoing organisational restructuring was still treated as an association of banks). Competition authorities frequently and *expressis verbis* considered interchange fees too high compared to underlying costs. In the course of the proceedings, card schemes argued that they qualify for an exemption under Article 101(3) TFEU. However, their argumentation was most often not accepted by competition authorities. Visa and Mastercard failed to prove that interchange fees as a mechanism for balancing cardholder and merchant demands resulted in a more efficient production or distribution of goods, in technical and economic progress and in consumers receiving a fair share of benefits. Note that according to the European Commission's guidelines on the application of Article 101(3) TFUE, the concept of consumers should be understood more broadly and encompass merchants, or possibly other economic agents involved as direct or indirect users of the product; a payment card in this case (Börestam and Schmiedel 2011: 33). Thus, the guidelines took account of the two-sided markets theory (see Chapter 1).

On many occasions, in response to antitrust investigations, banks or card schemes in Europe made concessions and lowered interchange fee rates, like e.g. in France, Italy, the Netherlands. This way banks and card organisations were able to avoid competition fines. Nonetheless, many of the cases ended in courts and typically the court battles have lasted years. The European Commission made a series of investigations against Visa and Mastercard. In Visa 2001, Visa 2002, Visa 2010 and Visa 2014 cases, the card organisation was conciliatory and made binding commitments accepted by the European Commission. In 2010 Visa committed to cap at 0.2% cross-border (intra-EEA) consumer debit card MIF rates and domestic consumer debit MIFs in the countries where cross-border MIF rates applied in absence of other domestic MIFs, and to improve the transparency measures, i.e. soften HACR, unbundle acquirers, publish interchange fee rates, make identifiable payments with commercial cards (ECN 2012: 13). In 2014 Visa extended its commitments to credit cards and capped at 0.3% the maximum weighted average MIF for consumer cards for intra-EEA payments (cross-border payments between countries of the European Economic Area). Mastercard was more combative than Visa. It appealed to court from the Commission's

2007 decision prohibiting MIFs on cross-border payment card transactions in the EEA but lost before the General Court, which upheld the Commission's decision. In September 2014 the European Court of Justice (case C-382/12P) confirmed that Mastercard's MIFs for cross-border payment transactions in the EEA restricted competition in the European Union and were in breach of the EU competition rules. Facing the pending judgement and serious fines, in 2009 Mastercard complied with the Commission's 2007 decision and, similarly to Visa, capped cross-border intra-EEA consumer debit and credit card MIFs at 0.2 and 0.3% respectively.

Not satisfied with the lengthy proceedings before courts, regulators in some European jurisdictions drafted bills on interchange fees (e.g. in 2013 in Hungary and Poland). Also elsewhere in the world, laws were passed targeting interchange fee rates and card scheme practises regarded as anti-competitive.

In Mexico a law became applicable in 2004, which gave the central bank of Mexico the powers to regulate retail payment systems, including the rate of interchange fees. The Bank of Mexico recognised their levels as a likely cause for the low card acceptance network and card usage in Mexico. The Bank of Mexico stated that it was not right to charge almost the same interchange fee rates for credit and debit cards and asked banks to change the practice, set a new methodology for determining the level of interchange fees and reduce interchange fee rates. In less than three years, between January 2004 and May 2006, they dropped significantly, credit card interchange fee levels from ca 2.45 to ca 1.80%, debit card interchange fee levels from ca 2.60 to ca 0.75%. As a result, merchant service charges for retail sales merchants and restaurants went down in this period from ca 5.3 to ca 3.0% for credit cards and to 2.2–2.6% for debit cards (Medina et al. 2007). The Bank of Mexico lifted HACR but not NSR. Merchants became allowed to accept only debit, credit or both types of cards. They could offer rebates for cash payments but not surcharge card payments (Weiner and Wright 2005).

In Canada the federal government engages in a dialogue with card networks. In 2010 the federal Department of Finance released the Code of Conduct for the Credit and Debit Card Industry in Canada. It brought a number of transparency measures, including the requirement for full disclosure of fees and rates in statements that acquirers present to merchants, 90 days' advance notice of fee increases, better identification of a premium card at payment terminals, merchant's option not to accept certain categories of cards, etc. The Code of Conduct is revised periodically and is in fact obligatory not voluntary, because if card networks do not accept its provisions, these can be enforced under the Payment Card Networks Act. The Financial Consumer Agency of Canada has the legal authority to overseeing whether card networks obey the rules of the Code of Conduct. In 2014, pursuant to its amendment, Visa and Mastercard agreed to decrease the weighted-average credit card interchange fee rates to 1.5% for five years, beginning in 2015. However, there are ongoing discussions, spurred mainly by merchants in Canada hailing Australia and the European Union as a model, aimed to make card organisations further reduce the ceiling on fees (Strauss 2017).

In Israel the Antitrust Tribunal looked at interchange fees and in 2006 it reached an agreement with banks to lower credit card interchange fee rates from 1.25 to 0.875% by 2012. In 2011 banks agreed to further decrease interchange fees from 0.875 to 0.7%. In 2015 the Bank of Israel decided to set a 0.3% interchange fee rate limit for debit card transactions for a one year period, starting on 1 April 2016 (Hayashi and Maniff 2017). However, in 2018 the Bank of Israel decided to accelerate the path of interchange fee reduction. Interchange fee rates will be brought down for credit cards in five steps from 0.7% in December 2018 to 0.5% in January 2023 and onward, and for debit cards in two steps from 0.30% in April 2016 to 0.25% in January 2023 and onward (Bank of Israel website, 25 February 2018).

In India the central bank intervened directly into merchant discount rates, not in interchange fees. Credit card merchant fees remained exempt from the regulation. Effective on 1 September 2012, the Reserve Bank of India (RBI) capped merchant service charges for debit cards at 0.75% for values at or below Rs 2000 and at 1% for values above Rs 2000. Aiming to promote debit cards, the RBI introduced even lower limits for merchant discount rates (RBI 2016, 2017):

- for smaller merchants 0.4% for physical point of sale and online transactions (Rs 200 cap per transaction), 0.3% for quick response (QR) based card acceptance infrastructure (Rs 200 cap per transaction),
- for larger merchants 0.9% for physical point of sale and online transactions (Rs 1000 cap per transaction), 0.8% for QR-based card acceptance infrastructure (Rs 200 cap per transaction).

In addition, the RBI moving towards less cash economy made a decision to waive entirely the merchant discount rates for amounts up to Rs 2000. For two years the RBI will reimburse banks for 0.4% of the payment amount in all merchant categories. The law became effective in January 2018.

In China, the People's Bank of China began to reform card fees already back in 2002 when it demanded from banks to provide merchants with more clarity on merchant fee components (interchange fees, scheme fees, acquiring fees) and set maximum merchant rates differentiated by merchant types. Effective February 2013, next reductions of merchant fees occurred, by one-fourth (Hayashi and Maniff 2017). The last capping of fees, this time interchange fees not merchant fees, was put in force on 6 September 2016. The new regulation substituted for the previous one. The debit card interchange fee was capped at 0.35% of the payment value and a credit card interchange fee at 0.45% of the payment value. The central bank of China defined also the maximum absolute level of the debit card interchange fee at 13 renminbi. Moreover, it also limited the rate of payment network service charges on both debit and credit transactions to 0.065% of the payment value paid in equal proportions by card issuer and merchant. Certain types of merchants (e.g. hospitals, schools, universities) could qualify for a full waiver of all issuer and payment network service charges. Acquirer fees were not regulated (Wang 2016).

Table 6 summarises only selected cases of public authorities' involvement in card payments, analysed in this paragraph. In all continents interchange fees have been investigated as the source of possible market failure. Hayashi and Maniff (2017) list more public authorities' actions taken against interchange fees. The overall global trend has been towards reducing their rates. Typically, interchange fees are the ones to be brought down, more often than merchant discount fees. The history shows that pure antitrust proceedings against interchange fees are lengthy and less efficient, therefore public authorities resort to more direct measures by passing laws or authorising central banks, possibly other public institutions, to impose limits on interchange fees. On the other hand, four-party card schemes, faced with threats of fines or regulations, decide to lower fees, soften the rules such as "honour-all-cards" or "no-surcharge" and become more transparent in their scheme pricing policy towards merchants. Regulators choose to cover debit and credit cards, but in some countries—for various reasons—only debit or credit cards become regulated (see Table 6). Looking at interchange fee reforms, Americas tend to accept higher rates while Europe, Asia and Australia go for regulating interchange fees at a lower level.

Table 6 Global outlook on selected public authorities' involvement in card payments

Country	*Types of regulated cards*	*Caps on interchange fees*	*Transparency and other measures*
France	Debit, credit	On average 0.3% (2011), then 0.28% (2013)	Yes
EU (competition cases)	Debit, credit	On cross-border intra-EEA payments for debit 0.2%, credit 0.3% (2009–2014)	Yes
Mexico	Debit, credit	Quasi voluntary changes for debit from ca 2.60 to ca 0.75%, for credit from ca 2.45 to ca 1.80% (between January 2004 and May 2006)	Yes
Canada	Credit	Weighted-average 1.5% for a period of five years (2015–2020)	Yes
Israel	Debit, credit	For debit from 0.30% in 2018 to 0.25% in 2023, for credit from 1.25% in 2011 to 0.5% in 2023	Yes
India	Debit	Cap on merchant service charges, 0.75 or 1% (2012), ranging between 0.3 and 0.9% (2018)	Yes
China	Debit, credit	Caps on merchant service charges (2002, 2013), caps on interchange fees for debit 0.35%, for credit 0.45% (2016)	Yes

Source Own compilation based on various sources (see main text)

2.2 Regulation of Interchange Fees: Country Cases

This section explores three cases of countries where interchange fees became regulated. All three interchange fee reforms were undertaken in the twenty-first century. Australia began to intervene in the card payment market in the early 2000s, similarly did Spain with major changes scheduled in 2005. The US reform took place later, in 2011. In this section reforms' details and their outcomes are explained with reference to the conceptual framework developed in Chapter 1 (Sect. 1.2.5 "Framework for Assessing the Impact of Interchange Fee Regulation", hereafter "Framework").

2.2.1 *Australia*

The Reserve Bank of Australia (RBA) has been reforming the domestic credit and debit card market for the last two decades with the aim to improve the Australian payment system's efficiency and to promote competition in the payment services sector. The RBA introduced the reforms in a number of stages, performing initial interventions in 2003 and 2006. Prior to the first reform, the central bank of Australia consulted the Australian Competition and Consumer Commission (ACCC). In 2000 they published the joint study on interchange fees and access related to debit and credit card schemes in Australia (RBA and ACCC 2000). In this report they specified major issues hindering the growth of the domestic payment system: high interchange fees (higher for credit cards) that are not justified by the level of operating costs, unsatisfying rate of development in debit cards compared with credit cards, no-surcharge rule, restrictions on access to international card networks.

These problems were remedied by the following measures. The 1998 Payments System (Regulation) Act vested powers to regulate interchange fees and the payment systems in the RBA. Over 2003–2004 the Australian central bank:

- imposed the 0.5% weighted-average interchange fee cap on Mastercard and Visa schemes (for consumer and commercial cards),
- removed card networks' restrictions forbidding merchants to surcharge card transactions,
- opened access of non-financial institutions to card schemes, including the ability for retailers to self-acquire their own (on-us) transactions.

In 2006 the RBA concentrated on debit cards (considered more efficient than credit cards):

- revised the interchange fee limits for debit card payments in the way that decreased the difference between international card schemes and the domestic EFTPOS PIN debit card system (an interchange fee rate for international four-party schemes was reduced to 12 cents per transaction paid to the issuing bank and, for the EFTPOS system, to 4–5 cents per transaction paid to the acquiring bank),

- abolished honour-all-cards rule, merchants would be allowed to accept debit cards within a scheme without being forced to accept credit cards or vice versa,
- improved access to the bilateral EFTPOS PIN debit system for issuers and acquirers.

In addition, Visa and Mastercard were obliged to publish their interchange fees. Three-party schemes American Express and Diners Club committed to remove NSR along with four-party schemes.

The RBA assessed the reform effects. It published the review report in 2008 where it stated on the basis of the gathered statistics and market information that the regulation had achieved its goal. The price signals, price transparency and access regime had much improved (RBA 2008).

Figure 5 plots merchant fees for four-party schemes Visa, Mastercard and three-party schemes American Express and Diners Clubs.

Merchant service charges in Visa and Mastercard networks dropped significantly between March 2003 (prior to the reform) and December 2017 by around 60 basis points from 1.40 to 0.81%, which was more than the reduction in interchange fee rates for three-party schemes. In this period, merchant discounts for AmEx and Diners Club went down as well but by more modest 20–30 basis points and from higher levels. Later, however, when merchant fee declines in Mastercard and Visa schemes slowed down (see Fig. 5), the falls in merchant fees of three-party schemes were more radical, especially for AmEx (MSC in December 2007 stood at 2.15% while in December 2017 at 1.46%).

According to the RBA estimates, the reduction in merchant fees between November 2003 and December 2014 led to savings of around AUD 13 billion (RBA 2015: 23). The Australian central bank obtained this figure by comparing two scenarios, the first one reflecting the actual progression of average merchant service fee rates based on the total value of card transactions with the second one assuming that the average merchant service fee rates remained at their starting levels prior to the reforms (compare author's calculations for Poland in Chapter 3). If US merchant service fee rates were applied to the Australian number and value of card payments, then Australian merchants would pay AUD 4–4.5 billion more *per annum* (RBA 2015).

The RBA regulatory approach was intended to boost the development of debit cards compared to credit cards. This objective was achieved. After interchange fees regulation, debit cards were the fastest growing

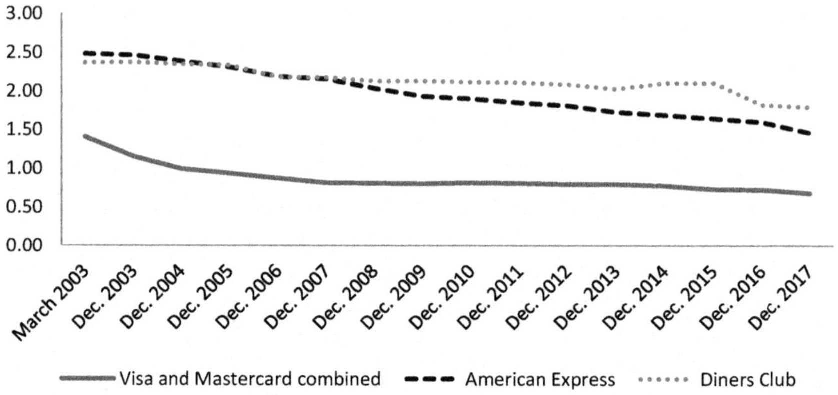

Fig. 5 Average merchant service fees in Visa/MC, American Express, Diners Club in Australia (in %) (*Source* RBA, payment statistics, Table C3)

payment instrument in Australia based on the number and value of payments. After 2006, growth rates of debit cards surpassed those of credit cards. According to the statistics from the RBA Payments System Board Annual Report 2012 (p. 9), the average annual increase in the number and value of debit card transactions in the period 2006/2007–2011/2012 was 14.6 and 12.8%, respectively. Credit card payments also grew, although at a slower pace. The average annual increase in the number and value of credit card transactions in the period 2006/2007–2011/2012 was 5.8 and 6.6%, respectively. In general there was no "death spiral" predicted by some opponents of the reform. On the contrary, the number of cards and the card spending continued their healthy growths (see area 1, claim 2 of the "Framework").

The RBA was never vocal about problems with expansion of the payment terminal network in Australia, unlike Spanish or Polish regulators (area 1, claim 1 of the "Framework"). The number of EFPOS terminals between 1990 and 2010 increased by almost 45 times. But year-on-year growth rates declined steadily from two-digits to one-digit 4% increase in 2003. In 2004 the growth rate went up to 7% (the time of caps on credit cards interchange fees in Visa and Mastercard networks coming into effect), in 2005 to 11%, then in 2006 down to 4%, in 2007 (after the capping of debit card interchange fees) up to 11% again, in 2008 to 10%, and then down in 2009 to 2%. After 2009 until 2017 the annual growth rates in card payment terminals fluctuated year after year at the one-digit level. Arguably, judging by these developments, declining merchant fees had a positive impact on card acceptance in Australia.

In reference to the question as to whether prices of goods and services fell in response to lower merchant fees (area 1, claim 3 of the "Framework"), it is important to note that econometric techniques can turn out imprecise taking account of many price drivers. According to the RBA, there are no grounds to deny that the savings from decreased merchant fees were passed on consumers in lower prices over the longer time horizon. Reductions in any business costs, that is wages, taxes, production costs must be passed through, provided the market is competitive (RBA 2015: 23). Previously, the RBA estimated that the cost savings in Australia stemming from the reduced interchange fees could likely lower consumer price inflation by around 0.1–0.2 percentage points over the longer term (RBA 2008: 23, see also discussion in Chapter 3 for Poland, Sect. 3.6 "Pass-Through Effect in the Holistic Perspective").

Improvements in price signals and in card fee settings should contribute to promotion of cost-efficient payment instruments. In Australia, there was competition not only in the credit card market but also in the debit card market. A domestic EFTPOS debit card system competed with four-corner international card schemes issuing debit cards. Initially, pursuant to the 2006 reforms, its interchange fee negotiated on bilateral basis flowed in an uncommon direction, from issuers to acquirers, and was capped at 4–5 cents (33–41% of the cap on Visa and Mastercard debit cards). However, the RBA noted that such a fee setting put its cost-efficient domestic debit card system at a disadvantageous position (see Chapter 1 for a discussion of reverse competition). Therefore, to ensure a level playing field, the RBA changed the regulatory regime in 2009 (with effect from 2010 onwards) to allow for multilateral interchange fees paid to issuing banks (subject to 12 cents ceiling), determined by ePAL—a newly established operator of the system. The system moved gradually to the multilateral fee setting and the average merchant fees for ePal system rose to around 9 cents in 2011/2012 (RBA 2012: 17). Nevertheless, its dominance over Visa and Mastercard debit cards was shrinking but still in 2012 it accounted for the majority of debit card payments in Australia (81 in number and 63% in value).

Detractors of the Australian reform warned that regulating four-party schemes of Visa and Mastercard would benefit three-party schemes of American Express and Diners Club (Epstein 2005). Indeed, in the first years after the reform, the market share of AmEx and Diners Club combined grew to a maximum in July 2011 by around 5% percentage points in the number of credit card payments (to 16%) and in the value of credit card payments (to 20.6%). However, in the longer term three-party schemes did not manage to keep the upward trend. In April 2018 their market share stood at 8.2% in number and 15.3% in the value of credit card purchases (RBA payment statistics), i.e. approximately the level as of the beginning of 2003 before the reform had taken place.

It is likely that American Express and Diners Club owed to the abolishment of the "no-surcharge rule" no long lasting success in increasing their market shares in Australia. Their cards, already subject to higher merchant fees, were also much more often charged merchant's add-on fees at the counter than cards of the competing four-party schemes—Visa and Mastercard. Gans and King (2008) argued there is no reason for the card payment market with strong externalities to set the optimal interchange fee with NSR in place. The RBA must have shared this view, because it opted to lift NSR and cap interchange fees.

However, to an extent unparalleled in any other country, Australian merchants used their new right to surcharge credit card transactions extensively. Large merchants were much more prone to steer consumers to low-cost payment instruments through additional fees at the till than small merchants (Chakravorti 2010). According to the RBA statistics, the share of surcharging merchants grew from a one-digit level in 2005 to 36% in 2012. Among the largest merchants in Australia more than 50% surcharged credit card transactions (RBA 2012: 25). Surcharging unmasked the costs of payment instruments in Australia, reflected differences in acceptance costs of payment instruments, exerted a downward pressure on merchant fees and contributed to the cost efficiency of the system but it showed also its dark side. Some of the merchants surcharged card payers excessively and practiced blended surcharging—applying the same surcharge to different types of cards with different interchange fee rates and merchant service charges (Wardrop 2017). The RBA cured this distortion by modifying the regulatory standard for interchange fees in 2016. It became effective in July 2017. Before, already in May 2012, the RBA allowed card schemes to limit surcharges to the reasonable cost of card acceptance (RBA 2015: 12). From July 2017 on, based on the amended provisions of the Competition and Consumer Act, all merchants in Australia have been prohibited to surcharge more than up to the actual average cost of acceptance linked to a particular card of Visa and Mastercard four-party schemes, domestic EFTPOS system or AmEx companion cards. AmEx and Diners Club in three-party format were left outside of the regime (Wardrop 2017: 113). There are penalties for breaching the ban on abusive surcharging.

In Australia American Express card started to be issued by banks as part of packages with a Mastercard or Visa credit card, with both cards having access to the same credit line (RBA 2015: 16). AmEx companion cards offer higher rewards than Visa or Mastercard cards within the package. In general, as an outcome of the interchange fee reform, the rewards on regulated credit cards became less generous. Still, some premium credit and even debit cards offer benefits. Cards with higher rewards are generally charged higher annual cardholder fees and have higher interchange fees applicable.

With regard to the pricing of bank products (see area 2, claim 4 of the "Framework" in Chapter 1), the RBA undertakes surveys of bank fees each year and it also collects data on domestic banking fee income from households and businesses. In Australia, debit card services are typically bundled with transaction account services. After analysing the RBA's data on domestic banking fee income (by calculating various statistics based on available data series) and scrutinising the RBA's studies assessing the reform effects, there are several conclusions to be drawn. Until 2003 the bank income on merchant fees exhibited double-digit growth rates. In 2004 it dropped by 17% and in 2005 by 2%. Afterwards it was rising until 2017 at the compounded annual growth rate of around 5%. The dynamics of household fees on credit cards and on transaction deposit accounts indicate that the fees increased temporarily, around the time of the reform, meaning that banks tried to offset the income lost on interchange fees. However soon after, the fees (and fee income) fell (see Fig. 6). In 2008 the banking income on household transaction accounts grew at ca 13%, but in 2009 it went down by almost 12% and in 2010 by more than 36%! Regarding consumer cardholder fees on credit cards, they grew quickly in 2003 and 2004 (by around 40 and 27%, respectively), but later the growth rates declined. In evaluating whether the growth rates in consumer cardholder credit card fees in 2003 and 2004 were unusually high, it needs to be mentioned that also before credit card interchange fees were capped to 0.5% in November 2003, those annual growth rates tended to be high (e.g. 36% in 1998, 34% in 2000, 25% in 2002).

Nevertheless, the structure of the Australian domestic banking fee income has changed, with credit cards and loans gaining, and transaction

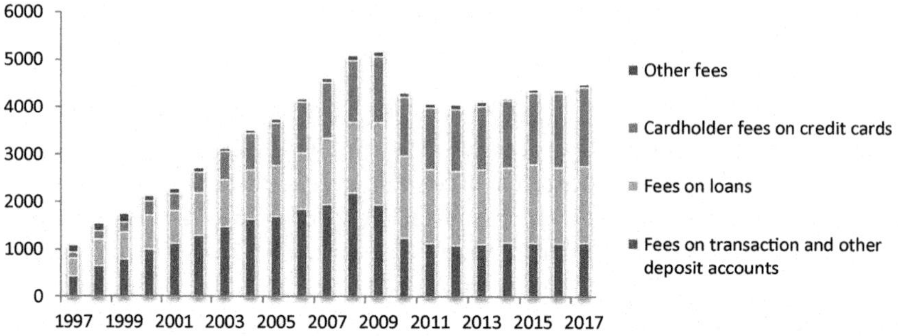

Fig. 6 Domestic banking fee income in Australia in the years 1997–2017 (fees from households in AUD million). *Note* Not included are exception fees (charged when the customer breaches the terms of a banking product, typically by making a late payment or exceeding a credit limit on a credit card or by overdrawing a deposit account) (*Source* RBA, payment statistics, Table C9)

accounts losing significance. The fee income from consumer credit cards accounted in 2017 for 37%, and in 2005 only for 24% of the household domestic banking fee income, whereas transaction accounts together with other deposit accounts (including bundled debit cards fees) in 2005 accounted for as much as 46%, while in 2017 only for 26% of the household domestic banking fee income.

The RBA estimates that over a longer period, the annual fees fell in real terms. The Bank warns at the same time that caution should be exercised when comparing annual fees of credit cards, because their population has changed substantially (2015: 17–18). The RBA's objective was to limit high interchange fees with no intention to harm the flexibility of the system. Therefore caps were set upon a weighted average interchange fees. Unfortunately with time, the system of interchange fees became really complex. Between 2003 and 2013 the number of interchange fee categories for credit cards at Mastercard increased from 3 to 19 and at Visa—from 5 to 23 with some rates as high as 2%. Over the same period, the number of interchange fee categories for debit cards in each four-corner system rose from 1 or 2 pre-reform to 15 post-reform (RBA 2015: 20–21).

Most probably, the complexity of the interchange fee system was one of the main reasons why the RBA, after reviewing the reform effects in 2015–2016, decided to establish a new cap on individual interchange fee rates at 0.8% for credit cards (with the weighted average benchmark remaining as it was to date at 0.5% but calculated quarterly rather than every three years). The new legislative package brought American Express companion cards, too, under the regulated interchange fee cap. Those changes together with the ban on excessive surcharging (discussed above) went live on 1 July 2017 (see the RBA website).

The initial 2003–2004 reforms improved the access regime for four-party card schemes, Not only banks but also supervised institutions, so-called Specialist Credit Card Institutions, could apply for Visa or Mastercard membership. International debit card systems and the domestic EFTPOS system became more open as well (RBA 2008: 8).

After the initial interchange fee reform, Australian merchants would make use of an option to let customers decide for dual-network debit cards which routing network to choose at the payment terminal: the domestic EFTPOS system or the international scheme system (RBA 2015: 33). One of the large retailers even disabled the international scheme routing network. Notwithstanding this fact, the domestic ePal system, favoured by merchants, had been steadily losing their share to international schemes' debit cards, as a result of reverse competition, that is higher interchange fees applicable to Mastercard and Visa cards making their issuing more profitable for Australian banks (RBA 2015: 16).

There is little information available about scheme fees' adjustments in Visa and Mastercard networks. Consultation reports suggest that a growing card usage together with some increases in scheme fees has strengthened the position of four-party schemes, positively affecting their profit and loss account (TransAction Resources 2011: 20–21, see area 3, claim 5 of the "Framework"). It is clear that interchange fee regulatory intervention has had no adverse impact on competition and innovation on the Australian payment market. Cash usage has been declining gradually and new methods of payments and form factors have gained popularity. Digital wallets of PayPal, MasterPass, Visa Checkout and many online methods of smaller payment service providers have emerged on the market. Like elsewhere, also in Australia contactless payments have developed as well as biometric methods of authentication and cryptocurrencies, including bitcoins (RBA 2015: 17). Earlier in 2018, real-time payments enabling money transfers in seconds were rolled out based on the New Payments Platform built by the biggest Australian banks.

2.2.2 USA

In July 2010 the US Congress enacted the Dodd–Frank Wall Street Reform and Consumer Protection Act, with one section sponsored by Senator Richard Durbin, whose intention was to give relief to businesses and consumers by decreasing the costs of high interchange fees. The Durbin Amendment instructed the Federal Reserve Board to regulate debit card interchange fees by setting them at a reasonable level commensurate with the costs of transaction processing. The FED published the rules, known as Regulation II or Reg II in June 2011 and they became effective on 1 October 2011.

Reg II consisted of several provisions (Hayashi 2013; FED 2016):

- cap on both signature- and PIN-authorised domestic debit card payments (to USD 0.21 plus 0.05% multiplied by the transaction value, plus a 1-cent fraud-prevention adjustment, if eligible),
- ban on "network exclusivity" arrangements between networks and banks and prohibition of "priority routing" (banks were barred from forcing merchants to route transactions through one network, thus merchants started to be able to select between several, at least two, networks for processing transactions, with no priority routing imposed).

The Board's original proposal was to cap debit interchange fee at a lower level than it eventually did, at 12 cents, which would better reflect the corresponding authorisation and clearing transaction costs. However, financial institutions succeeded in their lobbying efforts and the regulator set a higher ceiling fee (Shapiro 2013: 2). The cap was introduced only for large banks, with more than USD 10 billion in assets. Smaller banks remained exempt. Together with credit cards, all prepaid cards, whether issued by covered or exempt banks, as well as debit cards issued pursuant to government-administered payment programmes were left out of the Reg II scope and not subject to the interchange fee cap (FED 2016).

Reg II was accompanied by an antitrust settlement in July 2011 which relaxed discrimination rules in Visa and Mastercard schemes. They could no more restrict merchants' ability to offer rebates for the use of specific payments instruments, e.g. cash or cards whose acceptance is cheaper (Hayashi 2013: 92). In the following years "no-surcharge rule", as a result of court settlements, was further relaxed. However, American merchants were rather unwilling to exercise this new right. According to empirical research, neither cash and debit card discounts nor credit card surcharging was common in the USA. In 2012 they accounted for just around 1.2–1.8% of all transactions (Stavins and Shy 2015, for more information see Sect. 1.2.4 "Scheme Business Rules ("No-Surcharge", "Honour-All-Cards") and the Blending Practice").

In the USA card transactions are processed either through dual-message networks or through single-message networks. In dual-message networks, authorisation is separated from clearing, in single-message networks authorisation and clearing are combined in one message. Although both types of networks have been undergoing changes and offered new functionalities, causing the demarcation line to blur, the categorisation is still useful. Typically, dual-message networks, of which there are three in the USA (Visa, Mastercard, Discover), process signature-authorised debit card transactions, and fourteen other networks process PIN-authorised debit card transactions. Among them there are networks which belong to Visa (Interlink), Mastercard (Maestro) and Discover (Pulse).

In response to the regulatory cap in the USA, networks created a new, two-tier interchange fee structure (for covered and cap-exempt transactions). Interchange fees for covered transactions experienced substantial drops in 2012, for dual-message they more than halved (from USD 0.58 to USD 0.24), for single-message transactions they fell by around one third (from USD 0.34 to USD 0.23). Since then, until 2018, the average interchange fees for covered transactions have barely changed (Fig. 7). After the cap introduction, interchange fees for exempt transactions went down only a little and remained higher than for covered transactions. In particular, the average interchange fee for (signature debit) dual-message exempt transactions stayed high (above USD 0.50). Interchange fees for (PIN debit) exempt transactions have been falling gently until 2018 to USD 0.25, by no more than 1 cent yearly, on average. In 2017 exempt debit card transactions accounted for 37% of the total number and 36% of the total value for debit card transactions. These proportions were several percentage points lower than when the reform took effect in October 2011, meaning that smaller banks and credit unions (exempt issuers) have not taken away a debit card market share from bigger players (covered issuers).

However, the competition between covered and exempt banks and between networks intensified. Before Reg II, in terms of transaction

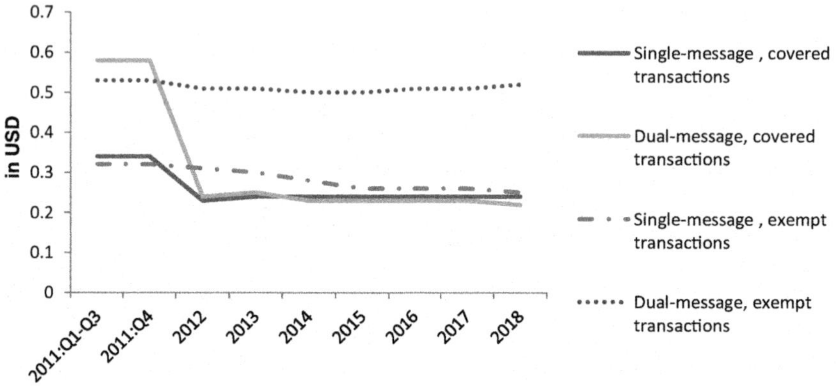

Fig. 7 Average debit card interchange fee in the USA (in USD) (*Source* FED statistics, FED website: section "Payment Systems", "Regulation II (Debit Card Interchange Fees and Routing)")

value, Visa's share constituted more than 60% of the entire market for signature and PIN debit card transactions combined (Hayashi 2012: 82). After Reg II in 2012 Visa's market share declined, judging by transaction volumes. Visa's PIN debit network Interlink lost to other PIN debit networks, such as: Maestro, Pulse, STAR. PIN debit card transactions became more evenly distributed between networks. Mastercard's combined (Mastercard + Maestro networks) share rose. Shifting shares suggest that merchants were consciously selecting cheaper networks, based on economic criteria (Hayashi 2012: 104–105). Initially, putting an end, through regulatory intervention, to exclusivity arrangements between banks and networks benefitted the market. However, large networks (with Visa first) sought ways to recoup their lower revenues and to strengthen their position against smaller rivals by introducing fixed fees paid monthly instead of per transaction fees. It decreased the transparency of network fees for merchants and made them limit their card acceptance to fewer networks.

PIN debit card transactions are considered more secure and cheaper in terms of underlying resource costs than signature debit card transactions. Hayashi (2013: 106) remarks, that after Reg II consumers appeared to start using PIN debit more often than signature debit as a consequence of the change in issuers' policy and more merchant steering towards PIN debit card use. Issuers withdrew from rewards for debit card users, especially for signature debit card users. However, it seems from looking at FED statistics that in the longer term, four years of Reg II becoming effective, dual-message networks have even gained a market share from single-message networks. In terms of transaction value, the first group accounted for 60% in 2011, while in 2015 for 65%.

There is no data collected by the FED on card payment accepting devices, so it is also not available in the data repository of the Bank for International Settlements (see BIS, Red Books). Fortunately, there are industry reports. North America held the largest share globally in the POS terminal market in 2016 (Grand View Research 2018). According to Medici Insights in January 2016 there were almost 14 million POS terminals in the USA. Following the liability shift in October 2015, the process of replacing old terminals with EMV-based more secure terminals picked up speed. In around six months until the end of 2015, the share of PIN-and-chip enabled terminals rose by 13 percentage points from 30 to 43%. 17% of all terminals were then equipped with the NFC contactless technology enabling Google Pay, Apple Pay and other proximity payments. Their development progressed afterwards. There is also visible strong trend of mobile POS terminals expansion in the USA. Special card readers (dongles) offered by different companies, like Square and SumUp, allow credit and debit card payments to be directly accepted on a smartphone through a dedicated app. In-app consumer-to-business and person-to-person payments through mobile wallet applications are becoming more popular.

The USA is the market from which payment cards originated. Before Reg II they had been accepted for decades and the card acceptance network had been growing constantly. In the context of recent developments, as it was explained above, there were probably other technological, social and regulatory factors influencing payment terminal growth and transformation more strongly than just lower merchant fees. Besides, the US public authorities regulated only debit card interchange fees, not credit and not (most of) prepaid card interchange fees. Therefore, direct effect of reductions in debit card interchange fees would be even more difficult to be isolated from other factors impacting the size of the card payment acceptance network (area 1, claim 1 of the "Framework"). On the other hand, there is no evidence against the positive effect of debit card interchange fee decreases on the payment terminal network. Interchange fee reductions must have supported its growth along with positive effect of other factors.

Card acceptance base fuels card transactions and card transactions drive growth in payment terminals. This indirect network effect exists also in the USA (compare area 1, claim 2 of the "Framework"). The question is whether debit card interchange fee decreases contributed to higher card use or maybe slowed down its development. It is also interesting to find out what types of cards were increasing faster.

In BIS Red Books (statistics on payment, clearing and settlement systems for CPMI countries) there is data on non-cash payment instrument usage. Countries can be compared under various criteria. The USA is characterised by strong development of non-cash payments. Regarding the number of card payments per inhabitant, with 326 in 2016 the USA was the leader among 23 countries listed in the comparison, higher than e.g. Australia and Sweden.

Table 7 shows that over the decade the number of cashless payment rose considerably. An average American made 460 non-cash payments in 2016 against 313 in 2006. Cash used in transactions has been declining steadily (not displayed in Table 7). Among non-cash payment instruments cheques lost much of their significance, all other payment instruments gained, but credit transfers and direct debits' share increased only a little. Meanwhile, payment cards enjoyed a strong growth. Their share in all non-cash payments (debit and credit cards combined) rose

Table 7 Number of non-cash payments per inhabitant in the USA, breakdown by type of cashless payment instrument for 2006, 2011 and 2016

	2006		*2011*		*2016*	
	Number of payments per inhabitant	*Share of the payment instrument (%)*	*Number of payments per inhabitant*	*Share of the payment instrument (%)*	*Number of payments per inhabitant*	*Share of the payment instrument (%)*
Debit card	87	28	157	43	212	46
Credit card	75	24	78	21	114	25
Credit transfer	20	6	25	7	33	7
Direct debit	29	9	38	10	50	11
Cheque	102	33	68	19	51	11
Total	313	100	366	100	460	100

Source Own calculations based on BIS Red Books

Table 8 CAGR of number and value of debit and credit card payments pre-Reg II and post-Reg II

	Pre-Reg II	*Post-Reg II*	*Pre-Reg II*	*Post-Reg II*
	2009–2011 (%)	*2011–2013 (%)*	*2006–2011 (%)*	*2011–2016 (%)*
CAGR of number of debit card payments	12	6	13	6
CAGR of number of credit card payments	3	7	1	8
CAGR of value of debit card payments	12	7	12	6
CAGR of value of credit card payments	7	7	2	7

Note Rounded and calculated based on tables "number and value of payments per inhabitant" from BIS Red Books; therefore there are small differences (around one percentage point) in comparison to calculations based on raw data on number and value of payments from FED statistics
Source Own calculations based on BIS Red Books

from 52% in 2006 to 71% in 2016. The midpoint of the time interval was in 2011, exactly when the Durbin Amendment was introduced. Taking into account the pre-Reg II and post-Reg II five-year periods, debit card payments growth slowed down, contrary to the growth of credit card payments, which accelerated.

The regularities detected are confirmed by calculations of compounded annual growth rates (CAGR) of number and value of debit and credit card payments. Calculations done for pre-Reg II and post-Reg II two-year and five-year periods shed more light on changing payment patterns (Table 8). The growth in credit card payments pre-Reg II was much slower than that of debit card payments. Credit card payments got impetus post-Reg II and started increasing faster than debit card payments. The latter also comprises prepaid card transactions which according to FED data constituted in 2017 about 6% of the total number and value of debit card payments. Another fact is that CAGR of debit card payments was twice higher pre-Reg II than post-Reg II. Apparently merchant steering towards debit card payments was not as effective as the policy of banks which induced more credit card payments in the US post-Reg II.

Manuszak and Wozniak (2017) examined how covered and exempt banks reacted to the regulatory debit card interchange fee caps and, more specifically, how account terms and fees changed (see area 2, claim 4 of the "Framework"). The study, based on the unique set of bank panel data from consultancy RateWatch, measured the effects over 11 quarters pre-Reg II and 11 quarters post-Reg II. The study did not look at credit card cardholder fees and rewards. Debit card cardholder fees were included to a certain extent by the investigation of monthly account fees, because American banks' policy in many cases was to bundle the two services (operate checking accounts and debit cards).

Banks responded in several ways. They increased, on average, monthly fees on non-interest checking accounts, interest checking accounts and saving accounts. Covered banks raised fees by around 20%. Interestingly enough, judging by equilibrium effects, exempt banks followed suit but with lower account fee increases. In both groups the availability of free accounts post-Reg II fell (by 35% at covered banks and by 15% at exempt banks). Manuszak and Wozniak detected also leading effects, which means that banks were reacting in advance, knowing that the Durbin Amendment would be put in force. Banks exploited the strategy of non-linear pricing by discriminating between account holders on the basis of whether they fulfilled given exempt criteria, i.e. most often whether they held sufficiently high account balances (compare the analysis of the Polish case in Chapter 3, Sect. 3.4 "Bank Profits and Cardholder Fees"). Smaller exempt banks and credit unions did not take the opportunity, failing to win the market from big banks, although there were some incidents temporarily threatening the position of high street banks but apparently with no long-lasting effect. On the famous "Bank Transfer Day", following the debit card interchange fee reductions on 1 October 2011, the Bank of America introduced a USD 5 debit card fee that caused people to switch their accounts to credit unions. It made the Bank of America cancel the fee.

Banks in the USA were motivated to offset lost interchange fee revenues. Based on FED data, in 2009 they earned USD 16.2 billion in debit card interchange fee revenues, two years later in 2011 the revenues totalled USD 20.4 billion. After Reg II was put in place, US banks' debit card interchange fee revenues declined by almost 25% year-on-year (USD 5 billion) to USD 15.5 billion. Afterwards in the years 2013–2015 they grew by an average of 6% annually to USD 18.4 billion in 2015.

Not all debit card transactions were subject to lower interchange fees. After Reg II, small-value payments of USD 5 or 10 (up to 15) became more expensive for merchants (Hayashi 2013: 94–95; Shapiro 2013: 15), because corresponding interchange fees were not decreased but actually increased to the maximum level permissible by Reg II. In addition, large merchants, which used to receive discounts for generating higher card payments volumes before Reg II, were deprived of these rewards post-Reg II. Thus all merchants, irrespective of their size, started to be treated the same.

In the USA, interchange fees accounted for circa 80% of merchant service charges (Shapiro 2013: 3). Overall, merchants received a relief from lower merchant fees amounting up to several billions of dollars in 2012. The issue that has sparked a heated debate is whether those savings were passed on to consumers as lower prices (see area 1, claim 3 of the "Framework"). There are clashing views in this respect among American economists. The pass-through rate in a not 100% perfect competitive merchant market could be lower than 100%. The actual pass-through rate from merchants to consumers is difficult, if not impossible, to measure although it is likely it has to take place, even if not instantly, due to the "rocket and feather effect" (more quickly when passing through cost increases than cost reductions, Hayashi 2013: 102).

Evans et al. (2013) did not engage in direct calculations gauging the impact of different factors, including debit card interchange fee reductions, on merchant prices but they used an indirect method: "event study". This technique assumes that it is possible to measure an event's effects through econometric modelling by examining company's stock exchange valuation. This method uses "wisdom of the crowds" from capital markets. According to the study results of Evans et al. investors anticipated that Reg II would increase retailers' and decrease banks' market capitalisation. The authors found that consumers lost more from bank fees' increases than they gained through lower prices and better merchant service. The present discounted value of the consumer losses throughout the lifetime of the interchange fee reductions totalled somewhere between USD 22 and 25 billion.

Shapiro (2013) used another method. He calculated "counter factual" interchange fees and the corresponding savings (compare the author's similar calculations in Chapter 3 and those by the Australian central bank in the previous paragraph in this chapter). In the absence of debit card interchange fee reductions, merchants (and ultimately the consumers) would pay USD 10.5 billion more in the first five quarters post-Reg II. Shapiro believes that the pass-through rate from merchants to consumers is around 70% following the empirical analysis of products and services prices performed by Nijs et al. (2009). In 2012, credit card interchange fee revenues for American banks totalled USD 26.2 billion. An average credit card interchange fee in the USA stood at USD 1.62 per transaction at that time. If credit card interchange fees had also been capped like debit card interchange fees at USD 0.24 per transaction, in 2012 alone American merchants and consumers would have saved USD 22.4 billion. Shapiro estimates that out of those savings USD 15.4 billion would have been captured by consumers and almost USD 7 billion by merchants.

The FED in its monitoring function has gathered, every two years since 2009, data on interchange fee revenues, covered issuer costs, merchant fraud losses related to debit cards. The reports do not include data on credit cards. Therefore it is difficult to assess the overall card schemes' policy. The reports, however, include one section devoted to network fees associated with processing debit card transactions (not covered are membership and license fees, FED 2016: 13). In 2015 acquirers and merchants paid USD 18.4 billion in debit card interchange fees to issuers. Networks collected USD 6.16 billion in network fees (out of this value 58% from acquirers and 42% from issuers). In absolute terms, the value of network fees has increased since 2009 and 2011 (introduction of Reg II), as a consequence of the rising payment volumes, but in terms of per-transaction value and percentage of transaction value, network fees have little changed (in 2015 USD 0.10 and 0.27%, respectively). Temporarily, they fell slightly in 2011. What changed is that acquirers/merchants started to pay more than issuers. The acquirers' share of network fees was 44% in 2009, 55% in 2011 and 58% in 2015.

In payments and incentives, the networks returned to issuers and acquirers USD 1.37 billion, out of this value one third to acquirers and two thirds to issuers. This proportion has not changed post-Reg II. The value of payments and incentives was lower than in 2011, when it amounted to USD 1.24 billion. However, on single transaction basis, the payments and incentives decreased a little, from USD 0.027 per transaction and 0.07% of transaction value in 2011, to USD 0.023 per transaction and 0.06% of transaction value in 2015. Therefore, based on available information (although not full, because of the missing data on credit cards and other types of scheme fees), there is no evidence that networks used the rebalancing mechanism to compensate issuers for lower interchange fee revenues by charging acquirers higher fees and redirecting them in compensation payments and incentives (see area 3, claim 5 of the "Framework"). On the other hand, in the USA there was no reason for doing so at all, because banks were motivated enough by no cap on credit card interchange fees and by the reverse competition in place, to issue credit cards and to nudge towards their usage through credit card rewards (possibly other favourable terms for e.g. grace period, interest rates, better service) and relative disincentives for debit card use. After the Reg II introduction, credit card payments indeed started to grow faster than debit card payments (see the statistics above for confirmation of this thesis).

The debit cards fraud rate grew considerably between 2011 and 2015 (by 63%) but most probably the shift to chip-and-PIN technology (more secure than magstripe) has already reversed this trend. With regards to innovation and competition on the US payments market, the FinTech revolution took place, even more intensely here than elsewhere in the world. Hundreds of start-ups were set up in the Silicon Valley and in other regions of the USA attracting huge funding. The payments industry has been flourishing with many solutions being rolled out and entering the market. Besides, in addition to Samsung Pay, Google Pay, Apple Pay, also other payment methods developed—see the success of person-to-person mobile payment applications: Venmo (PayPal-backed), Zelle (bank-backed) and Square Cash. A distinguishing feature of those applications is that they use different funding mechanisms, not necessarily card-linked, as in the case of Zelle, which operates on the basis of direct credit transfers between payer's and payee's bank accounts.

2.2.3 Spain

Regulatory interventions into interchange fees in Spain were first undertaken already in 1999 by the Ministry of Economy. Maximum interchange fees were reduced from circa 3.5% in 1999 to circa 2.75% in July 2002. In 2002 and 2003 the Spain's Antitrust Authority managed, through moral suasion, to decrease the maximum rates further, from 2.75 in July 2002 to 1.85% in January 2003 and to 1.75% in 2005. In December 2005 the most significant regulatory action took place, sponsored by the Ministry of Industry, Tourism and Trade which successfully promoted the agreement between payment networks and merchant associations to gradually reduce fees from 2005 to 2009 (Bank of Spain website and Carbó-Valverde et al. 2011). In setting of interchange fee benchmarks, only transaction processing and fraud costs within networks were taken into account. Decreases for debit and credit cards were scheduled differently for the years 2006–2009 (Carbó-Valverde et al. 2011):

- for debit cards the maximum interchange fee rates were set as a fixed amount at: EUR 0.53, EUR 0.47, EUR 0.40 and EUR 0.35 for 2006–2009 respectively,
- for credit cards the maximum interchange fee rates were set as a percentage at: 1.40%, 1.30%, 1.10%, 0.79% for 2006–2009 respectively.

Figure 8 displays maximum, average and minimum interchange fee rates for domestic (inter-network) card payments over the 2002–2011 time span. The most substantial drop in average interchange fee rates (for debit and credit cards combined) in Spain occurred between 2005 and 2006. There are three processing networks in Spain. Inter-network average interchange fee rates were higher than intra-network. According to rates calculated by Iranzo et al. (2012), average interchange fees fell from 1.55% in 2005 to 0.94% in 2006 and 0.77% in 2009. Average interchange fees for credit cards were lowered more than for debit cards. Between 2005 and 2009, the former declined by many basis points, while the latter just by several eurocents. Merchant service charges replicated roughly (but to a smaller degree) the pattern in interchange fee reductions.

The Spanish case attracts interest also because of the fact that it preceded the pan-European Interchange Fee Regulation in 2015 (see the next section for details). The first regulatory reforms capping interchange fees were undertaken already in the twenteith century and major reform took place in 2005, a decade before the EU Regulation became live. The analysis below focuses on the period when interchange fee caps were imposed and impacted the payments market transformation the most.

Figure 9 shows that the growth in the number of card accepting devices peaked in the period 2004–2008 (with maximum 16% year-on-year between 2005 and 2006), coinciding with the most significant decline in the interchange fee rates in Spain (see area 1, claim 1 of the "Framework"). The positive influence of the interchange fee reductions in Spain on merchant acceptance of card payments and usage of credit and debit cards (see area 1, claim 2 of the "Framework") is confirmed by an econometric study conducted by Carbó-Valverde et al. (2011, 2016)

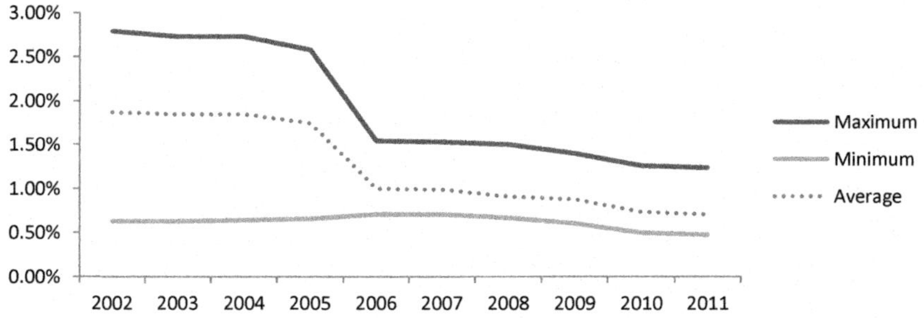

Fig. 8 Interchange fee rates for domestic payments in Spain (debit and credit cards combined). *Note* The methodology used for obtaining the interchange fees changed in Q2 2006. Therefore, in order to avoid distortions, the figures of the first quarter of 2006 have not been taken into account in the calculation of the annual fees for 2006 (*Source* Bank of Spain, payments data [interchange fees: inter-network transactions])

who used a simultaneous equations method, namely General Method of Moments, with acquirer and issuer specific fixed effects. The unique proprietary payment card data set of almost 2000 observations from 45 Spanish banks included different variables and consisted of quarterly time series from 1997 Q1 to 2007 Q4.

During that period, debit card transactions grew from 156 million to 863 million and credit card transactions, from 138 million to 1037 billion. The number of payments per card at card accepting devices rose from around 7 to 28. The number of payment terminals increased by more than half a million between 2000 and 2007 only (see Fig. 9). Carbó-Valverde et al. empirical study found that a 10% decrease in the rate of the average interchange fee reduction per quarter resulted in up to 1.4% rate of increase in merchant acceptance per quarter. Lower card acceptance costs induced more merchants to start accepting them. Furthermore, the researchers identified a positive indirect network effect consistent with the theory on two-sided markets, linking membership and usage externalities (compare in Chapter 1, Sect. 1.1.1 "Indirect Network Effects in Two-Sided Platforms"). The probability of point-of-sale transactions increases with the increase in the number of merchants accepting cards and the number of debit and credit cards issued. According to their study, a 10% growth in the rate of interaction

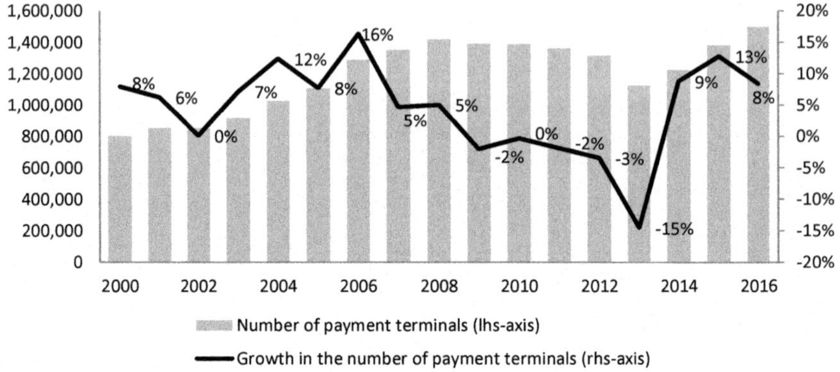

Fig. 9 Number of payment terminals and their growth rate in Spain (*Source* ECB Statistical Data Warehouse)

of merchant acceptance and the total number of cards raises the rate of quarterly issuer payment volumes by up to 1.7%. A growing merchant acceptance and number of cards, translating, to a certain extent, into more cardholders, boosted card usage.

Spain saw a great rise in credit card issuance and use at the time of falling interchange fee rates. Debit card also developed but not as quickly as credit cards. Actually, the number of debit cards fell between 2005 and 2010 from 31.8 to 28.6 million while the number of credit cards rose from 33.2 to 43 million (Iranzo et al. 2012, based on data from the Bank of Spain). The number and value of payments for both debit and credit cards grew, although faster for credit cards. Credit cards were subject to greater interchange fee reductions. Still, credit card adoption was higher even though credit card fees increased considerably. Iranzo et al. (2012) calculate that between 2005 and 2010 for the entire banking sector in Spain fees for credit cards increased by as much as EUR 715 million, whereas for debit cards only by EUR 141 million. Besides, also cost of credit incurred via credit cards rose by around 1.5 percentage point during the years 2005–2010 (from 12.5 to 14.0%).

Carbó-Valverde et al. (2011, 2016) study, as regards confirming rising credit card annual fees in Spain, is in line with that of Iranzo et al. (2012). Carbó-Valverde et al. suggested that debit card adoption might have reached a local saturation point. At the same time, credit cards became more popular. The researchers attempted to explain that demand for credit cards was quite price inelastic due to the indirect network effect, i.e. credit cardholders must have valued the growing merchant acceptance base in Spain more than they cared about rising annual fees. Another plausible explanation could be that banks were effective in persuading their clients to use credit cards through different promoting activities, including reward programmes. In a different empirical study, based on Spanish bank data, Carbó-Valverde and Liñares-Zegarra (2011) found that rewards are an effective tool of driving card use relative to cash use. Curiously, however, according to their study results, the impact of rewards on card usage is stronger for debit cards than for credit cards.

Carbó-Valverde et al. (2011, 2016) looked also at bank revenues. Acquiring side of the business was more impacted by the fall of interchange fees. Banks at the issuing side had more possibilities to respond to falling interchange fee rates, e.g. by raising the credit card annual fees. However, the main conclusion of the study in this area is that while per transaction bank revenues on card payments may have fallen, overall card revenues increased, because the increased value and number of payments compensated for the reduction in per transaction revenues (compare area 2, claim 4 of the "Framework").

Regarding the pass-through of savings from lower interchange fees to prices of goods and services, there is hardly any research available (see area 1, claim 3 of the "Framework"). This lack of research is also connected with the difficulty to disentangle the impact on prices the interchange fee reductions had from the impact of other factors, which are much more price-deterministic in magnitude. Iranzo et al. (2012) indicated that the merchant fees decreased in Spain less than interchange fees. Nevertheless, they were of the opinion that merchants kept higher margins for themselves. The researchers tried to support their opinion by referring to the results of the survey they conducted among merchant and consumer associations. Since most merchant associations refused to take part in the survey and most consumer associations responded that the lowering of interchange fees in Spain did not result in prices going down, the researchers concluded that there was no such price reduction. However, the method of opinion poll among consumer associations about the impact of interchange fee changes on prices of goods and services seems to make little sense. Therefore, there is no evidence that passing on savings from merchants to consumers did not take place in Spain. Instead, the more justified question would be whether the pass-through occurred in full, or in part, taking account of the degree of competition in the Spanish retail market.

Little is known about the details of the Visa and Mastercard scheme policy in Spain between 1999 and 2009 (see area 3, claim 5 of the "Framework"). Their cards, as in many other markets, dominate the card payments as well as all non-cash payments, leaving little space for three-party schemes (their share, mainly of American Express, oscillates around 1–2%). In terms of market split between Visa and Mastercard, the former is twice as big as the latter. Regarding transaction processing, three national payment networks operate in the country: ServiRed, Euro6000 and Telebanco 4B. Cash is king in Spain, but its use has been declining. Over the years 1999 and 2009 the growth in the number of cash withdrawals was lower than that of purchase transactions at POS terminals. However, the value of card payments first exceeded the value of cash ATM withdrawals in 2015. In 2016 cash accounted for around 80% of the total number of retail transactions (Clavería 2017). Innovation on the Spanish market has been present for many years. As a consequence of the global financial crisis, the country's economy experienced several years of low growth after 2009 but recently the economic situation improved. In October 2016 person-to-person mobile payments under the brand Bizum were launched with 27 banks providing this service (Clavería 2017). In November 2017 Spain was one of the countries starting to offer instant credit transfers in the pan-European format SCT Inst scheme (SEPA Credit Transfer Instant), developed under the auspices of the European Payment Council. Contactless payments are advancing in Spain, although in 2018 they were not as popular as in the UK, Poland or Czech Republic.

2.2.4 *Summary Comparison and Impact Assessment*

Three countries have been studied according to the "Framework for Assessing Impact of Interchange Fee Regulations" (Chapter 1) and more in-depth, paying attention to many detailed aspects of the reforms. In setting a benchmark for interchange fees, the cost-based approach was used in all three cases. Although this method has been criticised for looking only at issuer costs, and not at the demand side of the market and thus the welfare of consumers and merchants, it still proved to be useful in finding a rational benchmark for interchange fees. A method that is more grounded in the theory of two-sided markets, the tourist test (merchant indifference test), was recently adopted by the European Commission to determine suitable caps for interchange fees that are closer to socially optimal levels (see next section for the analysis of the EU Interchange Fee Regulation).

In Australia and Spain regulators intervened more widely in the card payments market and brought both debit and credit cards into the scope of interchange fee reforms. The US-public authorities were more conservative in their approach and capped only debit card interchange fees for large banks. Credit card maximum interchange fees were set as a percentage of the payment value, whereas debit card maximum interchange fees were defined as a fixed per-transaction amount or using a formula combining the two components: fixed and *ad valorem*. Weighted-average interchange fee caps allow for more flexibility within card schemes in setting interchange fees for different types of cards but, as the Australian case shows, they result in proliferation of interchange fee categories for debit as well as credit cards and a complex overall interchange fee structure. Probably this fact, among other factors, stood behind the RBA decision to cap also individual credit card transactions from July 2017 onwards.

Table 9 compares the interchange fee reforms in Australia, the USA and Spain and gives an overview of the regulations' impact, comprising all stakeholders, network effects, issues related to competition and innovation on the payments market.

Australian and American reforms of the card payments aimed not only at capping interchange fees but they also attempted to restrict anti-competitive business rules within four-party card schemes that the latter used for exerting market power. Relaxing or abolishing NSR and HACR increased visibility of payment instruments' costs to end users. Merchants were equipped with more tools for steering consumer choice towards payment methods where acceptance is less expensive. Through discounts, surcharges or simply by deciding which cards to accept or not, merchants' ability to signal the costs of different means of payment to consumers increased. Moreover, four-party card schemes were prohibited from imposing rules on priority transaction processing routing. Relaxing access regime to four-party schemes created more possibilities for new players to compete for clients.

In all countries capping interchange fees resulted in falling merchant service charges. Falling merchant fees support the growth of card payment acceptance network. Lower costs of acceptance reduce or remove the entry barrier to card acceptance for merchants. In particular Spain was the country, where reductions in interchange fees influenced smaller merchants to

Table 9 Comparison of interchange fee reforms in Australia, USA and Spain

	Australia	*USA*	*Spain*
Scope	Debit and credit cards	Only debit cards	Debit and credit cards
Time of the reforms	Ongoing, major reforms in 2003–2004 (credit cards), 2006 (debit cards)	1 October 2011	1999–2009 (major reforms in 2005)
Interchange fee caps (per transaction)	0.5% weighted-average interchange fee cap for credit cards (2003), AUD 0.12 for four-party schemes debit card payments, AUD 0.04–0.05 for domestic debit card EFTPOS system (2006), later changed to AUD 0.12, 0.8% on individual interchange fee rates for credit cards (2017)	USD 0.21 plus 0.05% per debit card transaction plus a 1-cent fraud-prevention adjustment, if eligible (on average 23 cents per transaction)	Stepwise decreases of maximum interchange fee rates 1999–2002, 2002–2003, 2003–2005 and finally progressive reductions over 2005–2009 (to maximum EUR 0.35 per debit card transaction and 0.79% per credit card transaction on 2009)
Other transparency measures	NSR and HACR lifted, non-discriminatory access to four-party schemes, more flexibility on network routing	NSR gradually relaxed, ban on exclusivity network arrangements and priority routing	Not known
Impact of transparency measures	Positive, improved price signals at merchant points-of-sale offering an efficient choice of payment instruments, excessive surcharging limited in extent (and remedied in 2017), improved access regime to four-party schemes (beyond incumbent banks), merchants benefited from more freedom in network routing	Positive, better cost transparency of payment methods (although to a limited extent due to relatively low propensity of American merchants to offer payment methods' discounts or surcharges), more competition between processing networks, competitive pressure on the largest Visa and Mastercard processing networks	Not known

(continued)

Table 9 (continued)

	Australia	*USA*	*Spain*
Impact on merchant service charges	Positive (average MSC decreased)	Positive (average MSC decreased)	Positive (average MSC decreased)
Impact on card acceptance	Slightly positive	Neutral or slightly positive	Positive (strong evidence)
Impact on card usage	Positive (healthy growth of card payments overall, increased use of debit cards compared to credit cards)	Positive overall (continued healthy growth of card payments), negative in that credit card use intensified more than debit card use	Positive overall (continued healthy growth of card payments), negative in that credit card use intensified more than debit card use
Impact on prices	Positive (arguably)	Clashing views and research	Hardly any research available, clashing views
Impact on bank revenues and cardholder charges	Bank revenues on interchange fees decreased, fee income on credit cards gained significance in the fee-based banking income in longer term, card rewards reduced, temporarily around the time of the reforms fees on cards and deposit accounts increased a little and so did the bank income but then they declined, competition within the banking sector suppressed increases of cardholder and accountholder fees	Bank revenues on interchange fees decreased, banks managed to get clients to use credit cards more relative to debit card usage, banks increased account fees, introduced non-linear pricing, reduced debit card rewards, increased interchange fees for small-ticket debit card payments, probably banks were successful in offsetting most of lost debit card interchange fee revenues	Per transaction bank revenues on interchange fees decreased but aggregated card revenues of banks increased due to the compensation effect of higher transaction volumes, credit rewards reduced, credit cardholder fees increased

(continued)

Table 9 (continued)

	Australia	*USA*	*Spain*
Impact on four-party card schemes	Positive in the long term, increased revenues, temporarily negative in that around the time of the major reforms the market share of three-party schemes increased but nevertheless recently four-party schemes strengthened their position	Positive in the long term, competition between networks increased, around the time of reform Visa's share for dual- and single-message networks fell, but then Visa and Mastercard adopted its pricing policy adequately, and their market and financial standing even improved	Positive in the long term, Visa and Mastercard did not lose market share to any other competing card scheme, little is known about their scheme fees but most probably schemes' overall revenues increased due to growing transaction volumes
Impact on competition and innovation	Positive, competition enhanced between three- and four-party schemes, different innovative solutions (e.g. companion cards), expansion of contactless payments, new form factors, tokenisation, biometric authentication, bitcoins, real-time payments	Positive, competition between dual- and single-message networks increased, thus Visa and Mastercard became subject to more intense network competition, competition between covered and exempt banks increased, although apparently smaller exempt banks and credit unions did not use the opportunity to win market shares from bigger covered banks, innovation in mobile P2P payments and contactless payments, EMV, NFC and mobile payment terminal network transformation, FinTech industry expansion	Positive, inter-network competition intensified, bigger pressure on cost-efficient processing, stronger growth of card payments relative to cash, after global financial crisis economic slowdown in Spain boost in innovation (contactless payments, FinTechs' activity, rollout of P2P mobile payment system Bizum based on credit transfers, SCT inst launch)
Impact overall	Positive	Positive (arguably, with ample room for improvement)	Positive

Source Own compilation

start accepting cards, because in Spain merchant card acceptance was far from complete. In Australia and especially in the USA it was not the case. Card payments had been widely accepted before the reform. Regulators in those countries never verbalised that their objective was to trigger growth in card acceptance by lowering interchange fees. Instead their intention was to lower the cost burden on merchants and consumers, improve the card system's transparency and increase card usage.

In all three countries card usage continued their healthy growths or even accelerated after the reforms. In Spain a strong indirect network effect was detected. More card accepting merchants contributed to higher utility of cards for consumers and drove card usage. The process was self-reinforcing. In Australia debit card payments benefitted more from interchange fee caps. Their growth surpassed the growth of credit card payments, which was the RBA goal. According to studies on payment instruments' social costs (see, e.g., Schmiedel et al. 2012) credit cards are among the least socially efficient payment methods. Debit cards and cash are socially more cost-efficient. Social (or societal) costs are resource costs of producing payment services with given payment instruments. Social costs are calculated as the sum of internal costs of all parties engaged in the payment service (central bank, commercial banks, subcontractors, merchants, consumers) or alternatively as the sum of all parties' private costs after netting out cost items that constitute revenues of one party and external costs of another. Merchant fees are an example of those private (external) cost items which net out in the calculation of social costs. On the other hand, credit cards, despite their low social cost efficiency, are far more profitable for issuing banks than other payment instruments, including debit cards. For this reason credit card usage is promoted by issuing institutions. In Spain and in the USA the interchange fee reforms resulted in more credit card use relative to debit card use which can be viewed as a negative consequence of the interchange fee reforms. *Nota bene* cash usage in payments has declined, this trend prevailing in all the three countries. In the context of promoting cards that are more profitable for issuers, there has also been found evidence for reverse competition. Cards with higher interchange fees were more willingly issued by banks and their usage promoted. Unfortunately, in Australia reverse competition harmed also the domestic debit card EFTPOS system. Its fixed amount interchange fee rose and transformed into a multilateral setting similar to that of international four-party card schemes in order to make the system more attractive for issuers.

Originally, the interchange fee in the Australian domestic scheme was paid by issuers to acquirers, then it changed its direction into a typical one and began to be paid by acquirers to issuers.

In assessing the effects of interchange reforms, the question arises whether or to what degree banks are able to recoup their lost interchange fee revenues by increasing card holder, and possibly account holder fees, and whether consumer gain from growing card acceptance, better cost transparency and lower prices of goods and services is higher in magnitude than the possible cost burden from higher bank fees. Critical for passing through the interchange fees in both transmission channels (issuers → cardholders/consumers and acquirers → merchants → consumers) is the competition in issuing, acquiring and merchant markets and market frictions stemming, *inter alia*, from asymmetry of information and from the structure of the card system.

In all three countries, banks were not indifferent about falling interchange fee rates, which hit their fee-based income and profit and loss account directly. The first response of banks was to cut rewards on cards and raise card holder and possibly account—and other payment services-related fees. It seems, however, that in Australia, the fees increased only temporarily around the moment of the reforms and then declined owing to the competition in the banking sector. In Spain, per transaction card fees decreased but banks benefitted from the compensation effect of higher card transaction volumes, which helped them offset the lost interchange fee-based revenues. In Spain credit cardholder fees increased but it did not stop Spanish consumers from using credit cards. The opposite happened. Spaniards valued the indirect network effect more and increased the credit card usage. In Australia, the share of credit card revenues in total fee banking income has increased over the years. In the USA after the debit card interchange fee reform, smaller exempt banks and credit unions did not use the chance to take away clients from big covered banks. In both groups account fees increased. A leading effect was even identified. American banks introduced nonlinear pricing, altered terms of account and debit card holding in the way it made more difficult for consumers to avoid bank fees.

In each of the countries, cumulated savings resulting from lower interchange fees amounted to billions of dollars in actual terms and to a much higher amount in counterfactual terms, assuming that if interchange fee caps had not been introduced, then merchants and subsequently consumers would have been charged the higher fees over more years (for detailed values see the Australian and American cases above). Opponents of the reforms claim that savings are not being passed through from merchants to consumers, while proponents argue they are, in various ways, either directly in lower prices or the pass-through effect is spread over time, meaning that the prices of goods and services rise at a lower rate after the reforms (the latter being more probable). It is equally difficult to prove econometrically that the pass-through takes place or it does not, because interchange fees are only one price determinant and, compared to other price determinants, their price impact is rather low. Based on the economic theory and rational thinking, assessing the pass-through rate from merchants to consumers requires studying competition and frictions in merchant market. The question is whether savings are passed through from merchants to consumers in full or partly and what the dynamics are in particular markets, i.e. if the lower interchange fees are not instantaneously transferred in lower prices, then what time does it take prices to absorb lower merchant (and interchange) fees.

An interesting takeaway from the studies of the interchange fee and card payment regulations in Australia, USA and Spain is that in all the studied countries the position of Visa and Mastercard has not weakened over a longer term. It is true that competitive pressure on four-party schemes has increased. In Australia Visa and Mastercard for several years lost market shares to three-party schemes (American Express and Diners Club). Then, however, they regained their position. In the USA, competition between networks, fuelled by the ban on network exclusivity arrangements between banks and networks, deteriorated Visa's share of debit card transaction processing but both Visa and Mastercard were able to respond with adequate policy adjustments and, also with respect to credit cards, they even managed to improve their market standing. Owing to the increase in transaction volumes, revenues of Visa and Mastercard kept growing.

However, the wave of innovations brought by disruptive FinTech solutions is bound to result in stronger competitive pressure on Visa and Mastercard card business. The rise of alternative cryptocurrencies, such as bitcoins, its underlying blockchain technology and real-time payments based on credit transfers (like Zelle in the USA, Bizum in Spain or SCT inst in the European Union) may well have an impact on expansion of cards in the long-term. For the time being, however, the status of international four-party schemes seems not to be endangered. In reference to competition and innovation in a wider context, there has been no evidence at all confirming that the interchange fee caps contributed to more frauds or less innovation. Conversely, their impact together with more transparency measures such as lifting of NSR and HACR, priority network routing enforcement, discriminative access regime, have yielded good results on the payment market.

The overall impact of the interchange fee reforms in Australia, USA and Spain is positive. The US regulation raises some controversies, because of the problems that materialised there, in particular in the form of accountholder fees' increases and growing credit card usage. This could be remedied by applying the regulation also to credit card interchange fee rates, not only to debit cards. Exempting smaller banks from the interchange fee caps is also debatable. If the exemption was introduced to better position smaller banks, it did not produce the desired outcome, because big banks did not lose any market share to smaller banks post-Reg II. Visa and Mastercard originate from the USA and probably this factor also plays a role. The US regulators are more indulgent towards four-party schemes and high-street banks than regulators elsewhere in the world. Therefore, most probably, US public authorities were reluctant to regulate also credit card interchange fees.

2.3 Interchange Fee Regulation in the European Union

The European Commission strives to achieve a non-fragmented internal market within the European Union. One dimension of this strategy is to create a Single Euro Payments Area (SEPA) for all electronic payments, including cards. Multilateral interchange fees, ranging significantly in their level across Europe, and other controversial practices applied in international card schemes were explicitly mentioned by the Commission as a problem in the Green Paper issued in 2012 "Towards and integrated European market for card, internet and mobile payments". It was stated that high MIFs may hamper competition in the payments market by creating high entry barriers to low-cost card schemes and other payment instruments and by inflating costs for merchants and consumers.

Jonker (2016) correlated domestic interchange fee rates with the number of card payments per capita for the EU countries. The relationship was inversely proportional. Based on 2011 data it appeared that countries with lower card usage were characterised by higher interchange fee rates whereas countries with higher card usage (e.g. Scandinavia) experienced lower interchange fee rates.

The sectoral inquiries on retail banking and on payment cards conducted by the European Commission in 2006 and 2007 revealed that issuing of payment cards was a highly profitable business in all European countries, much more profitable than acquiring. Credit cards generated higher profits than debit cards. In 20 out of 25 studied countries credit cards would remain profitable for the issuing banking sector even without interchange fee revenues. Only ¼ of possible higher revenues from interchange fee increases would be passed by European banks on consumers in lower card holder fees, which was considered low pass-through (European Commission 2006, 2007).

After making an impact assessment, the European Commission came to a conclusion that a pan-European regulation on interchange fees was needed. The impact assessment showed (see, e.g., recital 19 to the Interchange Fee EU Regulation 2015/751) that a complete prohibition of interchange fees for debit card transactions would be the best option for card acceptance and card usage, benefitting mostly consumers and merchants compared to any other, higher interchange fee rate cap setting. However, the Commission decided to implement less rigid provisions for issuers. Making reference to the merchant indifference test (see Sect. 1.2.3 "Optimal Interchange Fees"), it capped debit card payments at 0.2% and credit card payments at 0.3%. Before the IF Regulation was published in the Official Journal of the European Union on 25 May 2015 and entered into force on 8 June 2015, it had gone through the entire process of public consultation involving the trilogue negotiations between the European Commission, the European Parliament and the Council of the European Union comprising all member states (Allix 2015).

2.3.1 Timetable, Scope and Caps

The IF Regulation became effective throughout the European Union in two stages. Six months after coming into force, that is on 9 December 2015, the caps on interchange fees became applicable. Most of the transparency and business rules applied after another six months, on 9 June 2016.

The European Commission brought into scope of the regulation all consumer card and card-based (mobile, wallet) payment transactions.

Only cards issued within the European Union were covered. The IF Regulation excluded from caps:

- transactions with commercial cards,
- withdrawals at automated teller machines and at the bank counter,
- transactions with payment cards issued by three-party schemes,
- instruments used in closed-loop systems within a limited network of service providers,
- instruments used to buy limited range of goods and services,
- instruments used in a single member state for special social or tax purposes.

Three party schemes licensing partners (with implicit interchange fees) were covered by the regulation, unless the member state implemented a national exemption option based on the premise that a market share of such a three-party does not exceed 3% of the value of all card-based transactions in that member state.

Regarding debit (including prepaid) card transactions, member states could choose and set an *ad valorem* or fixed interchange fee cap:

- 0.2% per transaction,
- 0.2% weighted average (applicable until 9 December 2020 only for domestic card payments),
- lower than 0.2% per transaction (for domestic debit card payments),
- fixed maximum fee amount (EUR 0.07),
- combination of *ad valorem* and fixed components (combined not exceeding 0.2% of the total annual transaction value of the domestic debit card transactions within each payment card scheme).

Regarding credit (including deferred debit and charge) cards, an interchange fee cap was set at 0.3%, with the possibility for member states to determine a lower limit for domestic credit card payments (cross-border intra-EEA credit card payment interchange fees would always be capped at 0.3%).

The IF Regulation stipulated a prohibition of circumvention, where a payment organisation acting to the advantage of issuers would make an attempt to compensate issuers for lost interchange fee revenues by extracting profits from acquirers through scheme fees (compare area 3 from Sect. 1.2.5 "Framework for Assessing the Impact of Interchange Fee Regulation").

2.3.2 Separating Scheme from Processing

The IF Regulation banned any territorial restrictions in card organisations licensing issuers or acquirers within the European Union. Besides, it obliged international card organisations to separate scheme and processing entities. The Commission's motivation was to prevent discrimination between processors. Banks and merchants should freely choose between different processing companies that best and most cost-efficiently authorise and clear their card transactions. It was envisaged by the regulation that until 9 June 2016 the technical interoperability between processing entities would be achieved.

The IF Regulation banned any scheme practices hindering co-badging, that is inclusion of two or more payment brands on one card or mobile wallet application. Payees (merchants) should have the right to choose at the till a default payment option out of the existing co-badged payment instruments but payers (consumers) should retain the right to override the pre-selection.

2.3.3 Other Business and Transparency Rules

The IF Regulation established also other business rules limiting the power of international payment organisations. In order to bring more transparency in card payments, acquirers shall offer retailers different merchant service charges for different payment card categories and brands with different interchange fee rates attributed (unblending). Merchant should become aware of each payment card category costs they bear. Blended rates would be allowed only at the merchant's explicit request in writing.

Honour-all-cards rule has been weakened. Merchants are authorised not to accept all cards within a brand, e.g. a merchant could accept Visa debit but decide not to honour Visa credit. Clients should be informed about the merchant policy of accepting certain categories of cards in a clear and unequivocal manner at the shop entrance and at the counter. However, if a certain category of cards is accepted, then a merchant is prohibited from discriminating between issuers; it cannot refuse any bank's card.

The IF Regulation puts an emphasis on steering mechanisms. Merchants have the right to influence customer choice of payment methods by non-financial steering, for example, informing clients about acceptance costs associated with different payment instruments or setting thresholds for card payments (European Commission 2015). Also, consumer's payment method choice can be steered by financial nudges, i.e. by rebating or surcharging. Rebates for using a particular payment instrument are allowed with no restrictions. With regard to surcharging, no cards subject to interchange fee caps can be surcharged by merchants based on the revised Payment Services Directive. This provision became applicable on 13 January 2018 (the day of PSD2 coming into force). Member states can extend the ban on surcharges also to three party schemes not covered by the IF Regulation.

Both the IF Regulation and the PSD2 give payees (merchants) an explicit right to obtain information on all charges applicable to specific payment instruments. According to the IF Regulation the information should indicate separately the interchange fees and other fees. In addition, merchants should be able to identify each card-based payment transaction.

2.3.4 Interchange Fee Regulation's Impact and Review Clause

Some member states, e.g. the United Kingdom went a step further in restricting card payments surcharging and extended the prohibition on charging additional fees to all consumer cards, also to American Express and Diners Club, that are willing to be treated as three-party schemes, thus beyond the scope of the IF Regulation. According to the empirical market study carried out in 2013 for the European Union member countries (see its results in Sect. 1.2.4 "Scheme Business Rules ["No-Surcharge", "Honour-All-Cards"] and the Blending Practice"), the Anglo-Saxon economies—the UK and Ireland—stood out in the European Union with the highest ratio of surcharging merchants, especially in such sectors as airlines, travel and hotels. In other EU countries, even if the ban on surcharging is not applied, merchants cannot charge more for the use of a specific payment instrument than the amount equal to costs incurred by the merchant for the payment instrument acceptance. This rule is laid down by the Consumer Rights Directive. As Valdis Dombrovskis, European Commission's Vice-President responsible for Financial Stability, Financial Services and Capital Markets Union put it in his speech of 12 January 2018 (on the eve of PSD2 becoming applicable): "...we are banning surcharges for consumer debit and credit card payments. This could save more than EU 550 million per year for

EU consumers…”.[1] On the other hand, according to the results of the “Study on the effects of information disclosure on consumer choice of payment instruments” of December 2013 conducted by the European Commission (2013b), surcharging was found to be a very effective tool driving cost-conscious consumer choices. The rebates turned out to be six times more effective than information-based transparency measures. In turn, the surcharges proved to be twice as effective as rebates. It seems right to state that as long as other payment instruments are accepted by surcharging merchants and the choice of a specific payment instrument subject to surcharge is not enforced by the merchant, the practice of applying a surcharge equal to acceptance costs brings positive outcomes.

The IF Regulation envisages three-party schemes to be treated the same way as four-party schemes if they use a co-branding partner or an agent. Again, in the United Kingdom, the Payment Systems Regulator (PSR) considered American Express to be a four-party scheme for domestic card payments. AmEx challenged this decision in court. In May 2016 the UK High Court of Justice passed on the case to the European Court of Justice which on 7 February 2018 confirmed the UK PSR decision and rejected the co-issuing interpretation of AmEx. This incident will have to be scrutinised by three-party schemes operating in Europe, such as AmEx and Diners Club. They will need to adjust their business models accordingly: either comply with all the IF Regulation provisions applicable to four-party schemes or organise the scheme in a manner to leave no doubt there is no licencing partner engaged and remunerated.

The IF Regulation mandated the European Banking Authority (EBA) to prepare draft Regulatory Technical Standard (RTS) establishing requirements with regard to separating scheme and processing activities within the payment scheme in terms of accounting, organisation and decision-making process. It took considerable amount of time to make the RTS applicable. The draft RTS was submitted by EBA to the European Commission on 26 July 2016. After more than one year of discussing and agreeing on its final form, the RTS was adopted by the Commission on 4 October 2017 and then, with no further amendments from the Council and the European Parliament, it was published on 18 January 2018. The RTS, specifying requirements to ensure functional independence of scheme and processing entities, entered into force on 7 February 2018. It defined rules for card networks regarding:

[1] http://europa.eu/rapid/press-release_IP-18-141_en.htm (15 June 2018)

- accounting (financial information, allocation of expenses and revenues, documentation of transfer of financial resources between payment card schemes and processing entities, review and frequency of financial information),
- organisation (functional separation in two legal entities or two separate internal business units, separation of workspaces, independence of senior management, independence of staff, remuneration, use of shared services, use of shared information management systems, sensitive information, code of conduct),
- decision-making process (independence of the management bodies, annual operating plan independence).

The IF Regulation has a review clause that obliges the European Commission to submit by 9 June 2019 a report on the application of the regulation to the European Parliament and to the Council of the European Union. Therefore, the European Commission published on 27 March 2018 a respective call for tender. The consortium selected in the tender procedure will have to assess the impact of all the IF Regulation provisions, including separation of card scheme from processing, payment sector evolution, development of fees and costs for payers and payees (two-sided market), merchant pass-through, exclusion of commercial cards, cross-border acquiring, the effects of co-badging, co-branding and other transparency measures (compare Table 10).

The report prepared under the auspices of the European Commission will make a comparison between two moments in time: before and after the IF Regulation came into force. The Commission already conducted the so-called zero study. For its purposes, data were collected from banks, card schemes and merchants.

There is already one study available on the impact of the Interchange Fee Regulation on merchants, with evidence from the Italian market. The econometric analysis was conducted by researchers from the central bank of Italy (Ardizzi and Zangrandi 2018). Using a panel of Italian banks, they found that in line with the regulatory intention, the interchange fee caps led to a considerable drop in merchant service charges and in turn to an increase in card payments' acceptance, measured as card transactions per payment terminal.

Table 10 Summary of scope and rules of the EU Interchange Fee Regulation

Scope	*Caps on interchange fees*	*Business rules and transparency measures*
• Covered domestic card and card-based payments in the EU area • Included consumer debit and credit cards • Excluded commercial cards • Specific exclusions (e.g. three-party schemes and ATM withdrawals)	• 0.2% for consumer debit card payments • 0.3% for consumer credit card payments	• Prohibition of circumvention (compensating issuers for lower interchange fee revenues through scheme fees or incentives at the expense of acquirers) • Ban on any territorial restrictions in the EU for licensing issuers and acquirers • Separation of payment card scheme and processing entities • Allowed co-badging and choice of payment brand or payment application (by merchants and consumers) • Unblending of merchant service charges • Abolished honour-all-cards rule • Allowed non-financial and financial merchant steering of consumer's payment instrument choice (allowed rebates, allowed surcharges for cards not subject to IF caps) • Obligation for acquirers to inform merchants on all individual card-based payment transactions

Source Own compilation based on the EU Interchange Fee Regulation 2015/751

In fact, the reform carried out on the pan-European level by the European regulator is probably the most complex one compared to any other reform (see above for cases of France, Mexico, Canada, Israel, India, China, Australia, USA, Spain and below for Poland). Perhaps the Australian regulation, taking into account its ongoing refinements, is most comparable in its scope to the pan-European regulation. In its impact assessment and for the purpose of the Interchange Fee Regulation review, the European Commission can benchmark against the conclusions from the studies conducted for Poland and other countries.

Bibliography

Allix J. (2015) *Regulation on Interchange Fees*, Presentation at the Payment Systems Market Expert Group Meeting, European Commission, Brussels, 28 April.

Ardizzi G., Zangrandi S. (2018) *The Impact of the Interchange Fee Regulation on Merchants: Evidence from Italy*, Questioni di Economia e Finanza (Banca D'Italia Occasional Papers), No. 434.

Börestam A., Schmiedel H. (2011) *Interchange Fees in Card Payments*, ECB Occasional Paper Series No. 131.

Carbó-Valverde S., Liñares-Zegarra J. (2011). *How Effective are Rewards Programs in Promoting Payment Card Usage? Empirical Evidence*, "Journal of Banking and Finance", Vol. 35, No. 12, pp. 3275–3291.

Carbó-Valverde S., Chakravorti S., Rodriguez-Fernandez F. (2011) *Regulating Two-Sided Markets: An Empirical Investigation*, Revised Version of Working Paper 2009–2011, Federal Reserve Bank of Chicago.

Carbó-Valverde S., Chakravorti S., Rodriguez-Fernandez F. (2016) *The Role of Interchange Fees in Two-Sided Markets: An Empirical Investigation on Payment Cards*, "Review of Economics and Statistics", Vol. 98, No. 2, pp. 367–381.

Chakravorti S. (2010) *Externalities in Payment Card Networks: Theory and Evidence*, "Review of Network Economics", Vol. 9, No. 2, pp. 1–28.

Clavería P. (2017) *The Spanish Payment Landscape: Innovation Gains on Tradition*, News & Insights, European Payments Council, 22 June.

Epstein R. (2005) *The Regulation of Interchange Fees: Australian Fine-Tuning Gone Awry*, "2005 Columbia Business Law Review", pp. 551–598.

European Commission (2006) *Interim Report I Payments Cards*, Commission DG Document, Sectoral Inquiry, Brussels, 12 April.

European Commission (2007) Report on the Retail Banking Sector Inquiry, Commission Staff Working Document, 31 January 2007.

European Commission (2012) *Green Paper: Towards an Integrated European Market for Card, Internet and Mobile Payments*, 11 January, Brussels.

European Commission (2013a) *Commission Staff Working Document (Impact Assessment for PSD2 and IF Regulation)*, SWD 288.

European Commission (2013b) *Study on the Effects of Information Disclosure on Consumer Choice of Payment Instruments*, Report, December.

European Commission (2015) *The Interchange Fees Regulation*, in "Competition Policy Brief" Occasional Discussion Papers by the Competition Directorate–General of the European Commission, Issue 3, June.

European Competition Network (ECN), ECN Subgroup Banking an Payments (2012) *Information Paper on Competition Enforcement in Payments Sector.*

Evans D., Chang H., Joyce S. (2013) *The Impact of the U.S. Debit Card Interchange Fee Regulation on Consumer Welfare: An Event Study Analysis*, University of Chicago Coase-Sandor Institute for Law & Economics Research Paper No. 658.

FED, Board of Governors of the Federal Reserve System (2016) *2015 Interchange Fee Revenue, Covered Issuer Costs, and Covered Issuer and Merchant Fraud Losses Related to Debit Card Transactions*, 30 November.

Gans J., King, S. (2008) *Where to Next on Credit Card Reforms*, "The Melbourne Review", Vol. 4, No. 1, May, pp. 42–48.

Grand View Research (2018) *Point-of-Sale (POS) Terminals Market Analysis Report*, San Francisco, USA.

Hayashi F. (2012) *The New Debit Card Regulations: Initial Effects on Networks and Banks*, "Economic Review", Fourth Quarter 2012, 79–115, Federal Reserve Bank of Kansas City.

Hayashi F. (2013) *The New Debit Card Regulations: Effects on Merchants, Consumers, and Payments System Efficiency*, Economic Review, First Quarter 2013, 89–117, Federal Reserve Bank of Kansas City.

Hayashi F., Maniff J. (2017) *Public Authority Involvement in Payment Card Markets: Various Countries*, August 2017 Update.

Interchange Fee Regulation (EU) 2015/751 of the European Parliament and of the Council of 29 April 2015 on Interchange Fees for Card-Based Payment Transactions, OJ EU L 123/1.

Iranzo J., Fernández P., Matías G., Delgado M. (2012) *The Effects of the Mandatory Decrease of Interchange Fees in Spain*, Study (Mastercard Commissioned Research).

Jonker N. (2016) *Regulating Interchange Fees for Card Payments*, In Górka J. (ed.) "Transforming Payment Systems in Europe", Palgrave Macmillan, pp. 149–181.

Manuszak M., Wozniak K. (2017) *The Impact of Price Controls in Two-Sided Markets: Evidence from US Debit Card Interchange Fee Regulation*, "Finance and Economics Discussion Series 2017-074", Washington, Board of Governors of the Federal Reserve System.

Medici Insights (2016) *Steady Growth in NFC POS Terminals in the US in the Last Six Months*, based on *US POS Market Analysis and EMV & NFC Status Review Report*, 12 January.

Medina R., Castellanos S., Mendoza A., Negrin J., Solis F. (2007) *The Mexican Experience on Interchange Fees*, Global Payments Week 2007, Salvador Bahia, Brazil, November 26–30.

Nijs V., Kanishka M., Anderson E., Hansen K., Krishnamurthi L. (2009) *Channel Pass-Through of Trade Promotions*, "Marketing Science", Vol. 29, No. 2, pp. 250–267.

Payment Services Directive (EU) 2015/2366 of the European Parliament and of the Council of 25 November 2015 on Payment Services in the Internal Market (PSD2), OJ EU L 337/35.

Reserve Bank of Australia (RBA), Australian Competition and Consumer Commission (ACCC) (2000) *Debit and Credit Card Schemes in Australia: A Study of Interchange Fees and Access*, joint Study, October.

Reserve Bank of Australia (RBA) (2008) *Reform of Australia's Payment System, Preliminary Conclusions of the 2007/2008 Review*, April.

Reserve Bank of Australia (RBA) (2012) Payments System Board Annual Report 2012.

Reserve Bank of Australia (RBA) (2015) *Review of Card Payments Regulation*, Issues Paper, March.

Reserve Bank of India (RBI) (2016) *Concept Paper on Card Acceptance Infrastructure*, 8 March.

Reserve Bank of India (RBI) (2017) *Rationalisation of Merchant Discount Rate (MDR) for Debit Card Transactions*, 6 December.

Schmiedel H., Kostova G., Ruttenberg W. (2012) *The Social and Private Costs of Retail Payment Instruments: A European Perspective*, ECB Occasional Paper Series No. 137.

Shapiro R. (2013) *The Costs and Benefits of Half a Loaf: The Economic Effects of Recent Regulation of Debit Card Interchange Fees*, Sonecon Report, 1 October.

Stavins J., Shy O. (2015) *Journal of Behavioral and Experimental Economics Merchant Steering of Consumer Payment Choice: Evidence from a 2012 Diary Survey*, "Journal of Behavioral and Experimental Economics", Vol. 55, pp. 1–9.

Strauss M. (2017) MasterCard Canada Sets New Tone in Fee Battle, "The Globe and Mail", 16 February.

TransAction Recources (2011) *Review of the Impact of Australian Payments Reform*, Federal Reserve System Docket No. R-1404, 22 February.

Wang V. (2016) *China Report: Uniform Interchange Rates Now Apply; Differentiated Interchange Fees Based on Different Types of Merchants No Longer Exist*, "Payment Law Advisor, Global Insights".

Wardrop A. (2017) *Dealing with Excess: Regulatory Perspectives on Surcharging for Payment*, University of Queensland Law Journal, Vol. 36, No. 1, pp. 99–118.

Weiner S., Wright J. (2005) *Interchange Fees in Various Countries: Developments and Determinants*, Payments System Research Department Federal Reserve Bank of Kansas City Working Paper 05–01.

CHAPTER 3

Empirical Investigation of the Polish Interchange Fee Reform Effects

This chapter concentrates on the impact assessment of the regulatory reductions in interchange fee rates in Poland. Three areas of concern are scrutinised according to the framework drawn up in Chapter 1. The analysis covers assessing the reform effects in two transmission channels: acquirer → merchant → consumer and issuer → consumer. The card scheme domain is discussed in the broader perspective, with references to the aspects of competition, security and innovativeness of the payments market.

The chapter starts with Sect. 3.1 describing the history of interchange fee reductions in card payments in Poland. Section 3.2 presents the results of two subsequent merchant surveys held in 2013 and 2014/2015, with special emphasis on the pass-through effect of decreases in interchange fee rates from acquirers to merchants. Afterwards, Sect. 3.3 examines whether and, if so, how strongly the card payments acceptance network and card usage reacted to lower interchange fees. Section 3.4 focuses on the reform's consequences for bank profits and for card- and account holders. Section 3.5 looks into the card scheme domain as regards rules and fees set by payment organisations and applied to issuers and acquirers. Section 3.6 centres again on the pass-through effect including consumers in the discussion and giving a more holistic perspective on the outcome of the interchange fee reform in Poland.

J. Górka, *Interchange Fee Economics*,
https://doi.org/10.1007/978-3-030-03041-4_3

3.1 History of Interchange Fee Reductions in Poland

For many years Poland was among European countries with the highest level of interchange fees (see Sect. 1.2.1. "Interchange Fee and Other Fees in Four-Party Card System" for cross-country comparison). This situation provoked discussions and protests of some groups. The skewed pricing strategy used by the platform on the two-sided card payment market makes consumers less sensitive towards card fees. Consumers are charged periodic cardholder fees. Typically, they are also not as well organised as companies or their associations. Merchants carry the burden of direct pricing on a transaction basis. For those reasons this group has traditionally been more active in opposing high swipe fees.

It was already back in 2001 that the Polish Organisation of Trade and Distribution (POHiD), representing large merchants, filed a complaint to the Office of Competition and Consumer Protection (OCCP) in Poland. Although the heart of the matter was high merchant discounts amounting at that time from 1.7% to as much as 4.5% of the transaction value, the OCCP formally addressed the multilateral method of fixing rates (price). In its decision from 29 December 2006, the OCCP recognised the banks' agreement for setting interchange fee rates as a coordinated practice restricting competition, and imposed a penalty of PLN 164 million on 20 commercial banks in Poland. Banks were also required to refrain from applying the practice. Before the decision was taken, the OCCP analysed the consumers and merchants' costs and benefits of interchange fees. The OCCP was not convinced by the banks' arguments that a fair share of benefits from interchange fees went back to clients and that interchange fee rates were set on objective criteria, thus fulfilling conditions for exemption under the antitrust law. Banks appealed against the OCCP decision to a court. First they won but then in 2010 the Court of Appeal annulled the judgement, sharing OCCP's arguments and referred the case back to the first instance court. Finally, after many trials, in 2015 the Court of Appeal ruled that banks were guilty of the concerted practice between undertakings and should pay the penalty. Banks applied for cassation to the Supreme Court in Poland, which in 2017 revoked the final judgement, announcing that some of banks' arguments should be reassessed. After more than a decade in courts, the case was again referred back to the Court of First Instance.

In the meantime, the interchange fee debate about the level of fees became more intense. The Polish central bank approached the issue several times and in 2011 it prepared a public report on the analysis of interchange fees in cashless transactions on the Polish market (NBP 2012). The report found that interchange fee tiers in Poland ranked the highest or among the highest in Europe, depending on the card type and on the payment network. The interchange fees represented up to 85% of the merchant service charge. In effect, high costs of card payments acceptance impeded the POS network growth rate, especially in less developed regions in the countryside and in small towns. NBP identified the discrepancy in the growth rates between the card usage and the acceptance network, the former being many times higher. Moreover, low-value payments suffered from high merchant fees.

Based on this report, the Payment System Council at the National Bank of Poland set up an Interchange Fee Task Force, which consisted of all card payments stakeholders. The Task Force met four times between November 2011 and March 2012 and drafted the "Programme of card charges reduction in Poland". The Programme proposed bringing interchange fee rates gradually down to the average EU level in 2012, i.e. to 0.70% for debit cards and 0.84% for credit cards. The target levels were to be reached in 2017. The Polish central bank sent the Programme for approval to payment organisations. Visa accepted it, Mastercard did not. Three-party schemes were out of its scope, as their operating model included no direct interchange fee. Upon failing to obtain a binding commitment from one of the payment organisations, Polish central bank made another attempt to execute the Programme by collecting signed declarations from issuing banks, acquirers and merchants. As a result of an insufficient support, this alternative attempt to find a market compromise failed, too.

However, the intense discussion around interchange fees and the public pressure began to reach their goal in another way. Payment organisations decided to revise their pricing tables with regard to fallback rates, e.g. in 2013 Visa reduced the interchange fee rate on debit card payments from 1.6 to 1.25% and Mastercard from 1.64 to ~1.11–1.32% (see Table 11). In addition, both organisations decreased interchange fee rates for public payments: Visa to a maximum flat rate of PLN 0.2 for debit cards and to PLN 0.3 for credit cards on 1 November 2012 and Mastercard to a maximum flat rate of PLN 0.18 for debit cards and to

Table 11 Overview of major changes in average interchange fee rates in Poland in the years 2012–2015

Card types and payment categories	*2012 (before reductions) (%)*	*1 January 2013 (%)*	*1 July 2014 (%)*	*29 January 2015[a] (%)*
Visa debit	1.60	1.25	0.5	0.2
Visa credit	1.45	1.30	0.5	0.3
Visa business[b]	1.60–1.90	1.60	0.5	0.2/0.3
Visa micropayments	1.60	0.90–1.00	0.5	0.2/0.3
Mastercard debit[c]	1.64	~1.11–1.32	0.5	0.2
Mastercard credit	~1.5	~1.32	0.5	0.3
Mastercard business[b]	1.70–1.90		0.5	0.2/0.3
Mastercard micropayments	~0.80		0.5	0.2/0.3

[a]For new contracts only; for old contracts there was a three-month transition period until the end of April 2015, [b]Debit and credit business cards combined, [c]Mastercard debit and Maestro combined
Source Own estimates based on Visa and Mastercard tables of interchange fee rates

PLN 0.25 for credit cards on 1 March 2013. At that time payment terminals were rarely installed at municipal, tax and other public administration offices. The reduction of interchange fees to such low tiers could have been regarded as an incentive for the rollout of public card payments. On the other hand, the volumes of such payments being insignificant, they did not affect bank revenues at that time. Other reductions of reimbursement fee rates introduced by Visa and Mastercard from 1 January 2013 (see Table 11) had a greater effect on banks, affecting their profit and loss accounts, but the impact was not yet large as compared to what happened afterwards (for calculations, see Sect. 3.4 "Bank Profits and Cardholder Fees").

Table 11 presents the scale of reductions of interchange fees that took place between 2012 and 2015. The 2014 interchange fee decrease to uniform 0.5% was much deeper than the one in 2013. Note that the table exhibits average percentage rates for unified categories of cards. In some cases, the two-part tariff interchange fee rate (e.g. in January 2013 for Mastercard credit 1.10% + PLN 0.19) was converted into an *ad valorem* rate by taking an average value of the card payment transaction at that time (PLN 94). For public payments, maximum interchange fee rates did not change after the regulatory reductions and could not exceed absolute levels set by payment organisations in November 2012 and in March 2013 (by Visa and Mastercard respectively). Payment organisations also defined absolute maximum rates of interchange fees (e.g. PLN 0.5) for other payment categories, such as: bill payments or courier services (the latter at Mastercard).

Starting in mid-year of 2012, a few months after the failure of the market compromise worked out in the "Programme of card charges reduction in Poland", the time was right to consider regulating interchange fee rates. Eight draft bills amending the Polish Payment Services Act were submitted to the Ministry of Finance or directly to the Sejm (the lower house of the Polish Parliament). Polish parties, the Senate (the upper house of the Polish Parliament) and also associations representing merchants prepared regulatory proposals for interchange fee reforms. They varied in scope and in the level of interchange fee caps.

Eventually, the law on interchange fees originating from the Senate proposal was passed by Sejm on 30 August 2013 and then accepted by the Senate on 20 September 2013. It came into force on 1 January 2014 but the uniform cap of maximum 0.5% of the payment value on all consumer and business cards became effective on 1 July 2014 after a six-month transition period given to issuers and acquirers to adjust their operations to the provisions of the new law. It envisaged more than just interchange fee caps, also various transparency measures (see Byrski 2014; NBP 2015). Payment organisations were obliged to publish their interchange fee rates and scheme fees as well as to inform the Polish Financial Supervision Authority about all the fee adjustments planned. Also, payment organisations were prohibited from imposing fees on transactions generated with other payment organisations' cards (before that, Mastercard used to collect fees for the Innovation for Poland programme not only based on the volumes of its own card payments, but also those of Visa). Positive steering mechanisms in the form of rebates were explicitly allowed by the new law but NSR and HACR were not much restricted. According to the law, newly established payment organisations would be excluded from interchange fee caps for a period of three years.

Soon after introducing the first interchange fee regulation in Poland, another one was passed as a direct response to the new rules on cross-border acquiring in the Visa payment network. The definition of cross-border acquiring changed. Domestic transactions processed by an acquirer from abroad in the EU would qualify from 1 January 2015 for 0.2/0.3% cross-border interchange fee rates. The Polish policymakers were afraid that large merchants could switch to foreign acquirers, thus weakening the competitive position of Polish acquirers. The legislative process was quick. It started in October 2014 and already on 28 November 2014, the bill voted on in its final form by the Sejm. The Senate adopted the law with no amendments on 4 November 2014. After the bill was signed by the President and published in the Official Journal in December 2014, there was a short *vacatio legis* and the new law came into effect on 29 January 2015.

The act provided definitions of debit and credit cards, merchant service charge and its components. A debit card definition also included prepaid cards. More transparency measures were introduced between acquirers and merchants. Acquirers were obligated to inform their merchants about any merchant service charge adjustment and about components of this charge (an interchange fee, scheme fees and an acquiring margin). Interchange fee caps further decreased, to 0.2% for debit cards and 0.3% for credit cards. However, new caps became applicable on 29 January 2015 only to new contracts between acquirers and merchants. For old contracts, the transition period for adjustments was extended for three months until 29 April 2015. Newly founded payment organisations could be exempt from the provisions of the new bill for two years longer than stipulated in the previous law on interchange fees in Poland, that is for five years (for more detail see Byrski and Marcinkowska 2015). The Polish legislator outpaced the Pan-European interchange fee regulation (IF Reg.), by introducing the 0.2/0.3% caps earlier. Under the EU IF Reg. caps became effective on 9 December 2015 and most of the rules on transparency, on 9 June 2016 (see Chapter 2).

3.2 Evidence on the Pass-Through Effect from Merchant Surveys

This part presents selected results of the two subsequent merchant surveys taken in 2013 (between September and November 2013) and 2014/2015 (between November 2014 and February 2015).[1] They help

[1] Merchant surveys were conducted as part of the research project of the Foundation For Development of Cashless Payments (FROB) and the Faculty of Management, University of Warsaw (WZ UW/FoM UW). The book's author was the principal investigator in

assess the pass-through effect from acquirers to merchants in a short term, i.e. up to eight months. The first survey covered 1052 and the second, 1000 merchants accepting cards for C2B (Consumer-to-Business) payments from seven branches of retail trade and services. The focus was on small and medium-sized merchants. Based on the employment criterion, merchants were categorised into employing up to 9 people, from 10 to 49 people and 50 people and more. The samples were statistically representative at the national level.

The first question at the stage of recruiting merchants to the survey was whether they accepted payment cards. In 2014, in all the studied sectors, around 1/5 merchants did so (Fig. 10). The share of merchants in retail trade was higher, ca 1 out of 4 merchants accepted cards. In the sector referred to as HoReCa (hotels, restaurants and cafes) in Visa and Mastercard terminology, the share of card acceptors in 2014 was 50% as opposed to 5% in the professional, scientific and technical activities section (e.g. photographers, translators, lawyers). According to the surveys' results, the 2 percentage point rise in card payments acceptance corresponded to around 13% merchants which started accepting cards over a year period between 2013 and 2014. The NBP data revealed even higher dynamics in the card acceptance network growth rate throughout 2014 (16%), implying that interchange fee decreases accelerated this rate.

Only every third merchant declared experiencing the regulatory reduction in interchange fees within eight months after 1 July 2014 (Fig. 11). Larger merchants were more likely than small ones to be positively affected by the reduction. The positive change impacted more companies than in the previous edition of the survey where merchants were asked if they had experienced the pass-through of interchange fee rate decreases self-introduced by payment organisations. Only about

the research project and its author. The project was funded by the FROB Foundation. Surveys based on the questionnaire prepared by the author were carried out by Ipsos market research institute using the CAPI technique (Computer Assisted Personal Interviews). Ipsos interviewed companies' employees responsible for the C2B (Consumer-to-Business) payments acceptance and having the knowledge about company finances. The study aimed, *inter alia*, at identifying: changes in the area of card acceptance and prospects of mobile payments and innovative forms of payments. This book shows only selected figures and tables from the survey covering the first aspect, with emphasis on the pass-through effect of the interchange fee decreases from acquirers to merchants in Poland. Ipsos prepared, under the author's supervision, two extensive reports (January 2014 and March 2015) in which all survey results are presented.

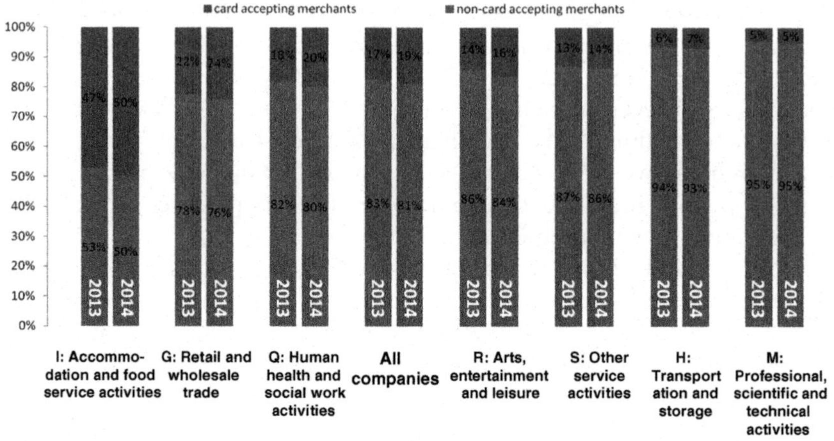

Fig. 10 Card acceptance in Poland (2014 vs. 2013) (*Source* Merchant surveys' results, $n=1052$ [2013], $n=1000$ [2014/2015])

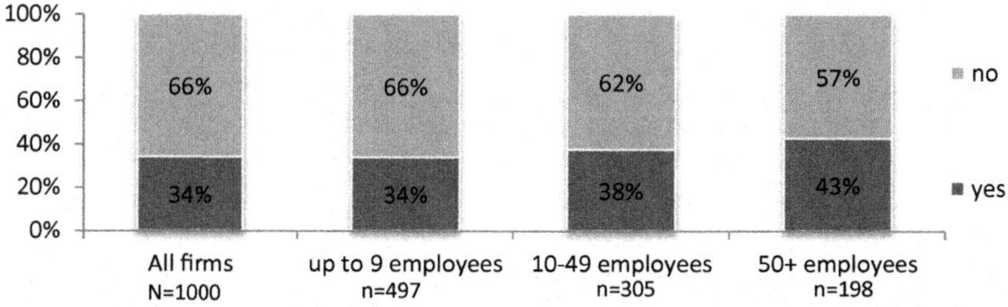

Fig. 11 Share of merchants experiencing the reduction in interchange fee rates after 1 July 2014 (*Source* Merchant surveys' results, $n=1000$ [2014/2015])

10% of merchants acknowledged it in 2013. Then, however, the vast majority of retailers (82%) were convinced that the upcoming regulatory reduction of interchange fee rates to 0.5% would make their costs of card acceptance decline. 48% of them expected the reduction not to be fully passed through by acquirers, whereas 37% were of the opinion that the transmission of lower merchant fees would occur with delay. On the other hand, 40% of companies awaited the instantaneous pass-through (with 23% undecided on the pace of the pass-through).

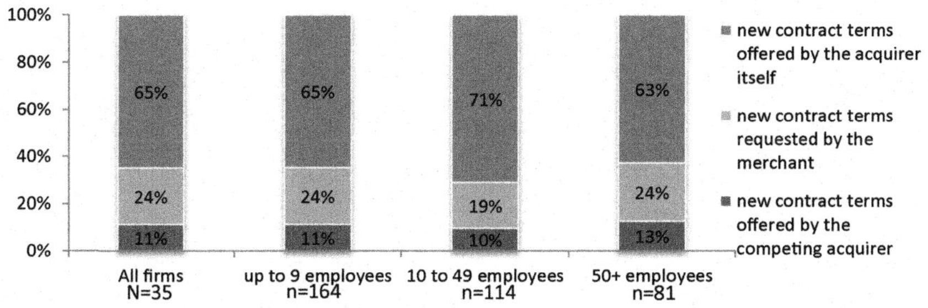

Fig. 12 The source of lower merchant fees (2014/2015) (*Source* Merchant surveys' results, merchants that experienced lower fees, $n = 359$ [2014/2015])

Among companies that noticed the reduction in merchant fees, 2/3 claimed that it was due to the initiative of the acquiring agent itself offering more favourable contract terms. One in four merchants (24%) experiencing the positive change in fees admitted it was an effect of its own effort, which means that better contract terms were requested and successfully renegotiated by the merchant from the acquirer. Only 11% of all merchants from the subgroup offered lower fees moved to another acquirer in the second half of 2014 and at the beginning of 2015 (Fig. 12).

It suggests that there must have been competition between acquiring institutions but in the short term they were benefitting from keeping higher margins in the segments of small and medium-sized merchants. On the other hand, when comparing results of both subsequent surveys, the share of merchants which migrated to another acquirer throughout their card accepting activity rose during the year by 3 percentage points, from 21 to 24%. Taking account of the increase in the number of card acceptors, it seems that the competition within the acquiring market was in fact rising, although potentially it could have risen more.

In the second survey, already after the regulatory reduction of interchange fees, only half of the merchants knew about the legislation bringing interchange fees down to 0.5% (63% of medium-sized companies accepting cards). Still, the awareness increased by 7 percentage points in comparison to the previous measurement (Fig. 13). In 2013, after the law on interchange fee limits was passed but before it became applicable on 1 July 2014, 43% of merchants had heard about the bill.

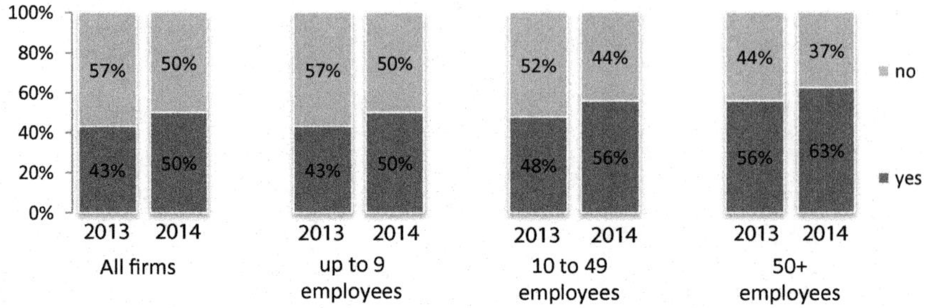

Fig. 13 Knowledge about the law capping the interchange fees at 0.5% from 1 July 2014 (*Source* Merchant surveys' results, $n=1052$ (2013), $n=1000$ [2014/2015])

In 2014/2015 the interchange fee regulation awareness correlated strongly with the readiness to switch from one acquirer to another with a better offer. In companies which changed at least once its acquiring agent during the card acceptance history (24%), respondents were significantly more often knowledgeable about the law capping interchange fees to 0.5% of the payment amount than in companies which never made such a decision (67–45%). It can be inferred that merchants which are better informed about market conditions relating to card fees and charges are more inclined to swap acquirers and to benefit from more favourable financial terms.

Respondents in 2014/2015 were divided in their opinions about the likelihood of other fees being introduced to compensate the decrease in interchange fees. 32% of merchants feared the increase of other fees, 32% were not sure of the future outcome and around 37% did not fear increases. Such a polarisation of answers clearly indicates the lack of certainty among merchants concerning the potential threat of circumvention of the regulatory interchange fee reduction.

All merchants with an IF+or IF++ structure immediately benefitted from the falling interchange fee rates. At the turn of 2014 and 2015 some large merchants, such as hypermarket chains, petrol station groups and big malls, were able to take advantage of pure IF+or IF++structures providing them with full transparency on all card types. However, as evidenced by the surveys covering small and medium-sized firms, blended MSC rates or partly differentiated rates for Mastercard and Visa cards were the norm in contracts with acquirers. As declared by

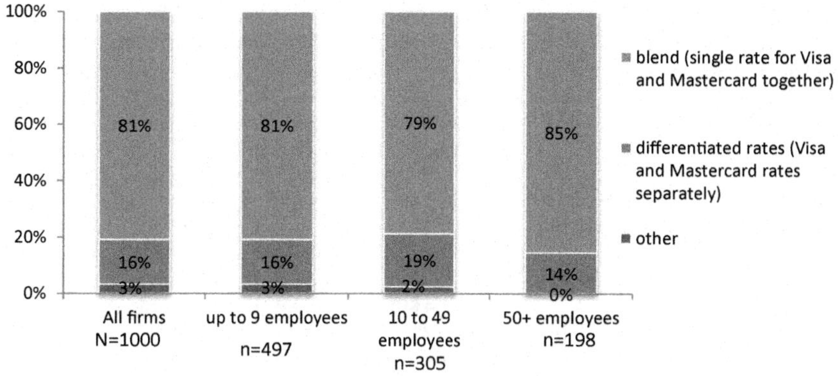

Fig. 14 Blending in merchant service charges (2014/2015) (*Source* Merchant surveys' results, $n = 1000$ [2014/2015])

merchants, in 2014/2015 (similar to 2013), 81% of them were subject to a blended MSC rate with no differentiation between cards of four-party schemes (Fig. 14). 9% of merchants included in this group claimed that their blended merchant service charge consisted of two parts: a percentage rate and a flat fee component (several groszy/cents). 13% of merchants declared differentiated rates for different card types of Visa and Mastercard, whereas 3% of merchants informed about a two-part tariff (16% in total). A few small companies claimed to have IF+/IF++ MSC settings (3%). In practice, these companies most probably can be included in the group of differentiated rates.

Table 12 demonstrates indicative levels of MSCs declared by merchants in the 2014/2015 survey. What strikes at first sight is that merchants which signed or renegotiated their respective contract with their acquirer after 1 July 2014, paid much less, i.e. almost half of the price compared to those merchants whose financial terms *vis-a-vis* acquirer had not changed (0.92% vs. 1.71% for a blended MSC rate). On average, taking into consideration contracts signed before 1 July 2014, merchants with differentiated MSC rates set out in their contracts with acquiring agents were charged lower transaction rates on their Mastercard and Visa payments than merchants subject to a single blended MSC rate (1.71% vs. 1.52% and 1.59%). According to the survey, the bundling of Visa and Mastercard payments together resulted in higher MSC rates but the rule does not apply to contracts signed after 1 July 2014.

Table 12 Average levels of blended MSC rates and Visa and Mastercard MSC rates for contracts signed before and after 1 July 2014 interchange fee reduction (2014/2015 survey)

Category	*Time*	*All firms*	*Firms up to 9 employees*	*Firms 10–49 employees*	*Firms 50+ employees*
Blended MSC rate	Before 1 July 2014	1.71% ($n=507$)	1.71% ($n=262$)	1.65% ($n=150$)	1.68% ($n=95$)
	After 1 July 2014	0.92% ($n=209$)	0.93% ($n=97$)	0.87% ($n=63$)	0.86% ($n=49$)
Visa MSC rate	Before 1 July 2014	1.52% ($n=85$)	1.52% ($n=47$)	1.55% ($n=26$)	1.49% ($n=12$)
	After 1 July 2014	0.90% ($n=27$)	0.89% ($n=13$)	–[a]	–[a]
Mastercard MSC rate	Before 1 July 2014	1.59% ($n=95$)	1.59% ($n=54$)	1.53% ($n=27$)	1.57% ($n=14$)
	After 1 July 2014	0.97% ($n=32$)	0.98% ($n=14$)	–[a]	–[a]

[a]Too few respondents (below 10); The blended MSC rate encompasses cards of Visa and Mastercard together. For merchants declaring differentiated rates, Visa MSC rates and Mastercard MSC rates are displayed separately. Some outlying or inconsistently declared rates were excluded from statistic calculations

Source Merchant surveys' results, $n=1000$ (2014/2015)

MSC rates are variable costs for merchants. There is also a fixed cost of a payment terminal that has to be paid regardless of the volume of card payments at the merchant's point-of-sale. Based on the 2014/2015 survey, the average terminal rental cost per month was PLN 56 net. The majority of merchants admitted that money from card payments is credited to their payment accounts within one or two business days (40 and 37% of the answers respectively). Around one-quarter of merchants (27%) expressed interest in the "no-surcharge rule" being prohibited by law. However, as a very limited number of Polish firms surcharge for card transactions, the abolition of NSR would most likely benefit them indirectly, that is by improving their bargaining power towards acquirers.

There is one major implication from the merchant surveys for the market impact assessment of the decreases in interchange fees with regard to the pass-through effect. Namely that not all card acceptors benefitted instantaneously from reductions, only those with IF+ or IF++ MSC structures. It means that large merchants were more likely to take advantage of lower fees than small and medium-sized companies in Poland, which were mostly paying blended MSC rates. Only ca 1/3 of small and medium-sized card acceptors experienced lower transaction fees after IF rates reduction on 1 July 2014 within the eight-month period. In 2013 the share was even lower (10%). The pass-through rate was affected by the awareness of card accepting merchants. In the 2013 survey, 43% and in the 2014/2015 survey, 50% of merchants knew about the regulation on interchange fees in Poland. It seems probable that, likewise, the non-card accepting population of merchants was not fully informed about the interchange fee reductions. This implies that the positive effect of lower interchange fees on the card payments acceptance network and on card usage in Poland was spread over time (the factor to be taken into account in econometric modelling, see next section below).

The interchange fee decrease reduced the barrier to start accepting cards. After 1 July 2014 the cost of merchant service charges was cut in half as evidenced by the 2014/2015 survey results. The competition within the acquiring market rose but acquirers were able to retain higher margins on those merchants which did not renegotiate or sign a new contract after 1 July 2014 (~2/3 of small and medium-sized card accepting merchants up to eight months after reduction). The competition for new merchants became more intense.

3.3 Card Payments Acceptance and Card Usage

Card payments are possible only in shops equipped with card accepting electronic devices. With no option to pay by card, consumers can only pay in cash. The absence of payment terminals at points-of-sale negatively influences the network effects related to card payments. Alongside with the Polish central bank, authors researching the issue in Poland also found that card acceptance costs constituted a major barrier for many merchants to begin accepting card payments (Harasim 2013; Maciejewski 2013; Górka 2013; Polasik 2015). The public criticism was mostly expressed about the level of interchange fees, which, according to NBP (2015), amounted to 85% of merchant service charges. MSCs on their part constituted, on average, 76% of all pecuniary costs of accepting payments cards (Górka 2012, 2013). For small merchants, fixed EFT POS rental costs could be also regarded as high and make them refrain from accepting card payments (Polasik 2015). The average share of the interchange fee in the MSC rose by 6 percentage points between 2008 and 2010 (NBP 2012; Maciejewski 2013). Merchants complained about the level of card acceptance costs. The price elasticity of non-card accepting merchant population to MSCs was high; companies expected decreases in MSCs as a condition to start accepting cards (Górka 2012). Based on those findings and on the theory (see Chapter 1), interchange fee decreases should result in a growing card acceptance and card usage. The section below studies this hypothesis.

Empirical data collected by NBP reveal the surge in quarter-on-quarter card acceptance and card usage growth rates in 2014 and 2015, when interchange fee reductions occurred (Figs. 15 and 16). Especially noticeable are quarterly card acceptance growth rates in 2014, when there was an unprecedented growth of merchants accepting card payments. Indicators in a few quarters surpassed 5% and the number of payment terminals in Q2/Q1 and Q3/Q2 2014 rose by 7.22% and by almost 6%, respectively. Note that in mid-2014 interchange fee rates were reduced to 0.5% of the card payment value.

Q/Q card usage growth rates are also visibly higher for 2014 and 2015 than in previous years. Suffice to note that, in two middle quarters of 2014, the number of card payments grew at a double-digit rate (by more than 12% in both quarters). Later, between Q2 and Q1 2015,

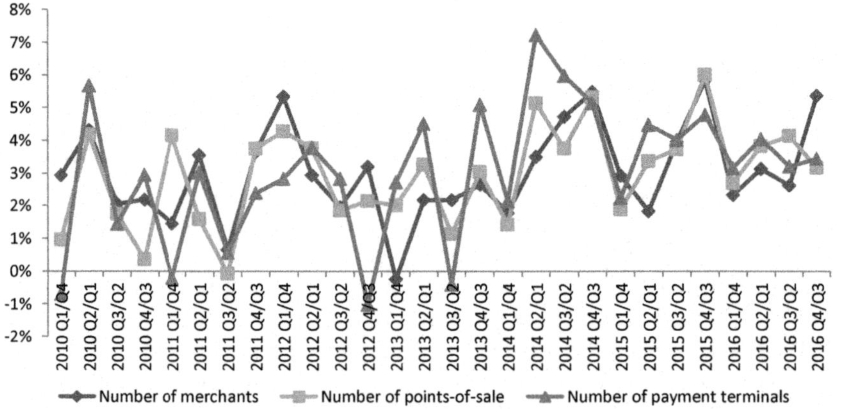

Fig. 15 Quarterly growth rates in card payments acceptance network in Poland (2010–2016) (*Source* Own calculations based on NBP data)

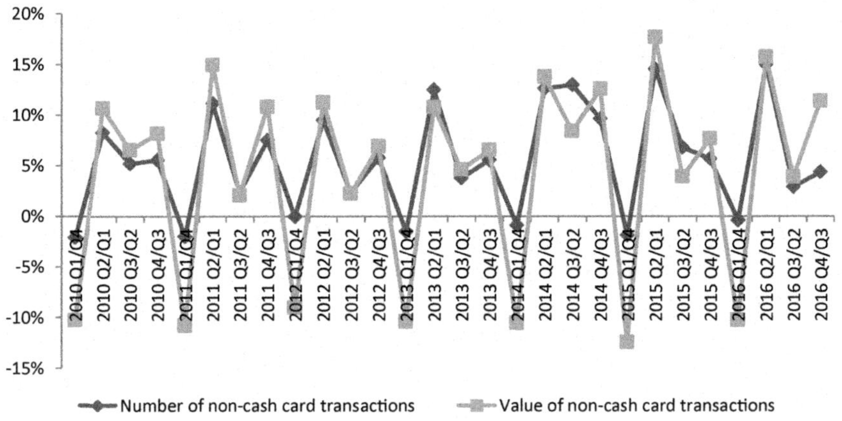

Fig. 16 Quarterly card usage growth rates in Poland (2010–2016) (*Source* Own calculations based on NBP data)

the value of card payments at brick-and-mortar shops grew by as much as nearly 18% (at the time of the second interchange fee rate decrease to 0.2/0.3%). These changes in card acceptance and card usage imply that reductions in interchange fee rates left a positive imprint. Harder evidence about the significance of these reductions for card acceptance and card usage in Poland can be found by using econometric techniques. Below, specific econometric models are estimated and compared to one another in order to extract the importance of the interchange fee decreases.

3.3.1 Model Selection for Time Series Modelling with Explanatory Variables

Investigating the supposed impact of the interchange fee reductions on the growth of the card acceptance network and card usage in Poland requires selecting a suitable class of econometric models. Seasonal Autoregressive Integrated Moving Average class of models has been chosen as fit for this type of analysis for a number of reasons. ARIMA models assume strong relationship between the value of a variable in one period and its values in previous periods. This is typical of such time series as e.g. the GDP, company's revenues (Makridakis et al. 1998) or time series exhibiting the size of the payments card acceptance network and card usage. SARIMA modelling involves decomposition of the time series into a trend, seasonal and irregular components. This type of modelling is also appropriate when there is a need to forecast accurately within a short time horizon based on shorter time series. Besides, SARIMA models may be used for examining the effects of a particular special event such as the interchange fee reduction, which was untypical in the past and may have affected the behaviour of a given variable beyond the previous pattern.

The Box–Jenkins methodology for ARIMA models was first described by the authors themselves in the early 1970s (1970). Further theoretical underpinnings were elaborated in detail in Box et al. (1994).

According to the Box–Jenkins methodology, each study should be broken down into three stages:

1. Stage I "Identification"—preparing the data (optionally, transforming the data to stabilise variation and differencing them to obtain stationary series) and selecting the model (data examination, ACF and PACF to identify potential models).
2. Stage II "Estimation and testing"—estimating parameters in potential models, selecting best models using different suitable criteria, and testing (diagnostics by checking ACF/PACF of residuals, doing various portmanteau tests of residuals and defining whether residuals are white noise).
3. Stage III "Application"—using the selected model to forecast.

Current statistical packages allow a smooth application of the procedure. When fitting an ARIMA model to a set of time series data, it is possible to use various techniques to minimise errors and to choose the one with the lowest Akaike Information Criterion (AIC), such as the Hyndman and Khandakar algorithm.[2]

[2]This algorithm is used in the R package in the auto.arima() function. "It combines unit root tests, minimisation of the AIC and MLE to obtain an ARIMA model. After determining the order of integration (the number of differences *d*) by using repeated KPSS tests, the algorithm employs a stepwise search to traverse the model space to select the best model with the smallest AICc" ("ARIMA modeling in R" https://www.otexts.org/fpp/8/7, 10 August 2018).

In general, the SARIMA models have the following notation (Makridakis et al. 1998: 346):

$$\text{SARIMA}(p, d, q)(P, D, Q)_s$$

where:

p (AR)—order of the autoregressive component
d (I)—degree of the differencing involved
q (MA)—order of the moving average component
P, D, Q—respectively p, d, q for the seasonal part of the model
s—seasonal lag

Simple notations can be converted into algebraic forms:

ARIMA(p, q)

$$Y_t = \underbrace{\phi_1 Y_{t-1} + \cdots + \phi_p Y_{t-p}}_{\text{AR}(p)} + \underbrace{\omega_t + \theta_1 \omega_{t-1} + \cdots + \theta_q \omega_{t-q}}_{\text{MA}(q)} + \gamma_t X_t$$
$$\Phi(p) Y_t = \Theta(q) \omega_t + \gamma_t X_t$$

ARIMA(p, d, q)

$$\nabla^d Y_t = \underbrace{\phi_1 \nabla^d Y_{t-1} + \cdots + \phi_p \nabla^d Y_{t-p}}_{\text{AR}(p)} + \underbrace{\omega_t + \theta_1 \omega_{t-1} + \cdots + \theta_q \omega_{t-q}}_{\text{MA}(q)} + \gamma_t X_t$$
$$\Phi(p) \nabla^d Y_t = \Theta(q) \omega_t + \gamma_t X_t$$

where $\nabla^1 Y_t = Y_t - Y_{t-1},\ \nabla^d Y_t = \nabla^{d-1} Y_t - \nabla^{d-1} Y_{t-1}$
X_t—regressor

SARIMA$(p, d, q)(P, D, Q)$

$$\boldsymbol{\Phi}(\mathrm{P}) \nabla^D \nabla_S^1 \left(\Phi(\mathrm{p}) \nabla^d Y_t \right) = \boldsymbol{\Theta}(\mathrm{Q}) \nabla_S^1 (\Theta(q) \omega_t) + \gamma_t X_t$$

where $\nabla_S^1 Y_t = Y_t - Y_{t-S}$
X_t—regressor

When needed, a SARIMA model can also be extended to include an additional regressor (X_t) or even multiple explanatory variables.

3.3.1.1 Data, Procedure and Assumptions

Modelled variables consist of two groups:

1. Group A representing the card accepting merchants' network, with three variables:
   - number of card acceptors (card accepting merchants),
   - number of card accepting points-of-sale,
   - number of card accepting devices (EFT payment terminals).
2. Group B representing the card usage, with two variables:
   - number of card payments,
   - value of card payments.

In group A, the number of card acceptors is the broadest category. Every merchant can have more than one point of sale and in every point of sale there can be multiple payment card accepting devices at the counter. As of the end of year 2016, there were on average 1.86 points-of-sale and 2.52 payment terminals per one card accepting merchant in Poland.

In group B, remote MOTOIO (mail order, telephone order, internet order) transactions were disregarded and removed from the dataset, only card payments at card terminals installed in physical points-of-sale were included in the time series for analysis.

It has been learnt from the merchant surveys that the effect of interchange fee rate reductions is spread over time (the pass-through effect, see the previous section "Evidence on the Pass-Through Effect from Merchant Surveys"). Even if an interchange fee reduction occurs in a given moment of time (e.g. in July 2014 when it fell most considerably, by more than 60% between the first and the second quarter of the year), its impact varies across the merchant population. Some merchants react in advance, preparing for the change while others (and this is a bigger group) react with delay. Therefore, the interchange fee as an explanatory variable should be smoothed to capture this specificity. In regression models, the interchange fee variable was smoothed (see Table 13) using a moving average of order 3 centred at time t (Y_{t-1}, Y_t, Y_{t+1}), reflecting the strongest relationship between adjacent quarters.

Time series of the data for group A and group B are published by Narodowy Bank Polski (the National Bank of Poland, NBP) with quarterly frequency. The Polish central bank collects the data for the number of payment cards issued since the fourth quarter of 1998, and for group

Table 13 A smoothed interchange fee variable over the years 2010–2016

Time period	*Interchange fee level (in %)*
2010 Q1–2012 Q3	1.6
2012 Q4	1.5
2013 Q1	1.4
2013 Q2–2014 Q1	1.3
2014 Q2	1.0
2014 Q3	0.8
2014 Q4	0.4
2015 Q1	0.3
2015 Q2–2016 Q4	0.2

Note Numbers rounded to one decimal place
Source Own calculations based on market data

A and group B time series, since the fourth quarter of 2003. The time series are pretty consistent in longer intervals. However, the NBP made some changes to the methodology of collecting the data from issuing banks and acquirers during that period. This should be borne in mind when comparing statistics between different years.

For this main reason, it was decided to narrow down the final analysis to the data from the year 2010 onwards. Another reason behind the decision was more empirical in nature. It turned out that models built on longer time series learnt the pattern from before the interchange fee reductions in 2014 and in 2015. Hence, the short-term forecasts they produced were not as accurate and as well fitted to the holdout set of the known historical data as those produced by models built on shorter time series. Eventually, the holdout set included last eight observations (eight quarters over years 2015–2016).

Time series were mathematically transformed using logarithms and normalised (by dividing the values by their historical maximum) in order to eliminate the problem of large numbers, to stabilise the variation and to make the process additive, so that the OLS or MLE methods would be easy to apply for estimating the parameters in a linear regression. Some of the variables exhibited a clear cumulated multiplicative trend (see figures below).

The procedure of building and selecting the models consisted in testing the fit quality and the forecast accuracy of all possible models with predetermined orders of the autoregressive and moving average parts. Models in which $0 \leq p,\ q,\ P,\ Q \leq 5$ were taken into consideration. It involved both the quarterly and annual seasonal dependency. Differencing, applied to remove the non-stationarity in a time series, was limited to two lags: $0 \leq d \leq 2$.

Simulations were conducted based on two generic sets of models. They were subsequently compared in how well they fit the empirical data in the training set and in the holdout dataset. The first set of models was pure SARIMA, the second set of models also included equations comprising the external interchange fee as an explanatory variable.

The quality of models was assessed against full diagnostics. Apart from checking the Autocorrelation and Partial Autocorrelation Functions of the residuals (ACF, PACF), Ljung–Box and Box–Pierce statistics were computed as well. The normality distribution of residuals was evaluated based on the Shapiro–Wilk test. Unit root tests were carried out to check for presence of the unit root in the autoregressive model. The best models were selected based on minimising the Akaike (AIC), the corrected Akaike (AICc) and Bayesian Information/Schwartz Criteria (BIC). All calculations were performed using the R package and the Forecast library. Models were selected on the basis of auto.arima() function using the Hyndman and Khandakar algorithm, combining the set of tests (see the previous paragraph for its explanation).

3.3.1.2 Time Series Examination and Identification

According to the Box–Jenkins methodology, each study should begin with the identification stage, where time series are initially examined, decomposed and checked for stationarity. Possible models can be identified. This paragraph ends with general conclusions about models. The best estimated models are presented in the next paragraph.

Figure 17 illustrates the original time series of six variables, three of which represent the card acceptance (group A), two—the card usage (group B) and the last one—the number of cards issued by Polish banks. All of the variables demonstrate a rising, mostly exponentially, trend entailing the need to use log transformation. Clear irregularities in group A time series can be observed around the year 2007, suggesting a change to the Polish central bank's data collection methodology. Although not so apparently visible from group A and group B time plots, the time plot for the number of cards reveals another irregularity in the year 2010, where the trend flattens abruptly. This is another argument behind the decision to narrow down the time period for analysis to data starting from the year 2010.

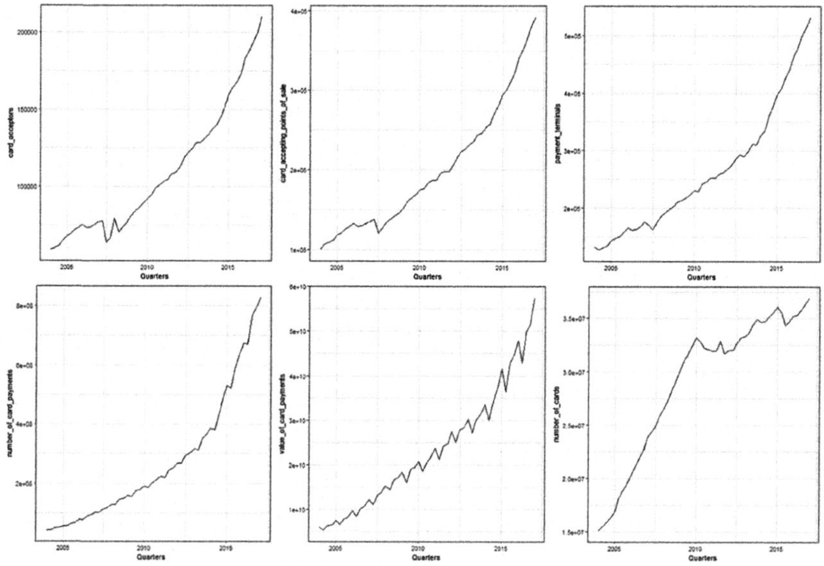

Fig. 17 Time plots for card acceptance network and card usage from 2003 4Q to 2016 4Q (quarterly data) (*Source* Own calculations based on NBP data)

Decomposition of all time series using moving averages enabled extracting the trend, seasonal and random components. Consider the time plot for the value of card payments at points-of-sale decomposed additively and multiplicatively, based on a non-transformed time series and a logarithmically transformed time series respectively (Fig. 18).

As Fig. 18 shows, there exist both a trend and a seasonal pattern. At some point of time around mid-2014 the trend line starts ascending more rapidly due to an external factor, presumably the change in interchange fee rates. Also, stronger fluctuations of residuals in an additively decomposed time series point at something unusual that must have taken place at the end of the analysed period. The remainders follow a white noise model better in a multiplicatively decomposed time series, suggesting that it is more justified to build models on logarithmically transformed data. In Fig. 18, seasonal aspects can be recognised as well, indicating quarterly and annual patterns.

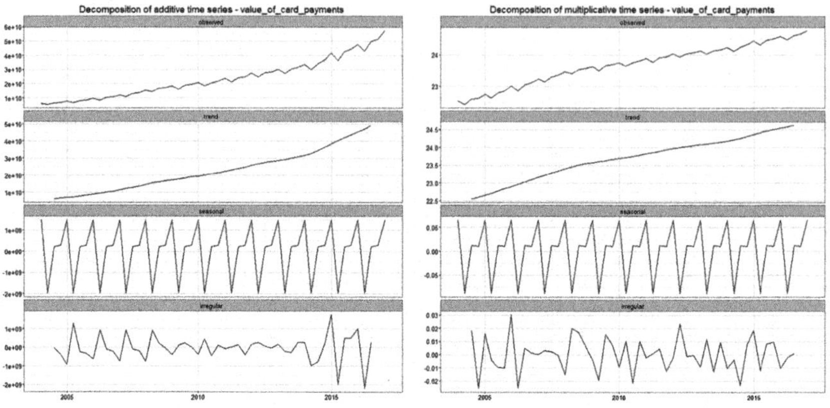

Fig. 18 Additive and multiplicative decomposition of the value of card payments variable (*Source* Own calculations based on NBP data)

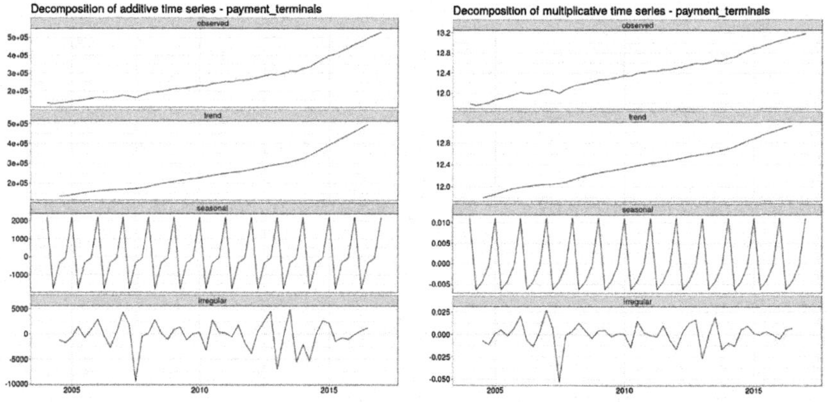

Fig. 19 Additive and multiplicative decomposition of payment terminals variable (*Source* Own calculations based on NBP data)

Similarly, a decomposition of other time series confirms what has been detected regarding the value of card payments, although there are slight differences between variables (see, e.g., Fig. 19).

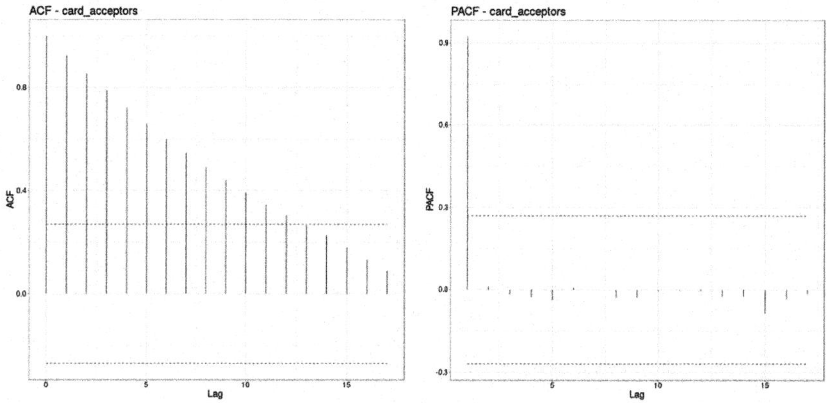

Fig. 20 ACF and PACF for card acceptors variable (*Source* Own calculations based on NBP data)

ACF shows that in some cases models must be built on differenced data, because the time series appears non-stationary (see Fig. 20). PACF may tell us whether there is a moving average part present.

Figure 21 depicts Autocorrelation Function and Partial Autocorrelation Function for the same variable (card acceptors) but built on logarithms and differenced once.

Time series for logged card acceptors is already stationary (see its ACF). ACF spikes more at lags 2 and 3 and PACF spikes at lags 2 and 5. Thus it could be inferred that there is an autoregressive component present (here even $t-2$) and there might be a moving average part.

In general, after investigating ACF and PACF for all the time series built on log-transformed data, it seems that models need differencing. Moreover, there are indications that models should have autoregressive parts. Some of them might include a moving average part, but it is not so evident.

3.3.1.3 Estimation and Testing

After decomposing time series in multiple configurations (differencing, data transformation) and examining their ACF, PACF, the models were estimated using the procedure built into the Hyndman and Khandakar algorithm combining unit root tests, minimisation of the AIC and MLE. Table 14 exhibits the best estimated models for the card acceptance

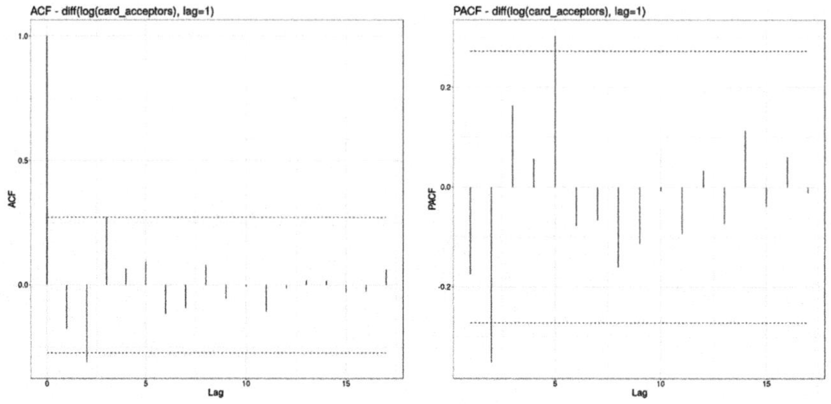

Fig. 21 ACF and PACF for logged card acceptors variable differenced at lag 1 (*Source* Own calculations based on NBP data)

network described by three variables and card usage described by two variables. In each case, two models were considered: one without and one with an interchange fee as an additional explanatory variable.

All identified models required differencing to produce a stationary process. The autoregressive term is a common part of the models. Often the values of a variable in the base period are related to the values in the period $t-1$. It means that there is a quarterly dependency. Card accepting points-of-sale exhibit mixed time properties, a non-seasonal, quarterly relation and the seasonal, yearly relation. Model specifications (SARIMA) confirm the yearly seasonality in number and value of card payments time series (see Sect. 3.3.1.2 "Time Series Examination and Identification"). There are almost no moving average parts in the models (q or Q), except for the payment terminal model (without IF). On the other hand, autoregressive coefficients are sometimes very high, such as 0.88 in the card acceptors with IF model. Not surprisingly, in models with the xreg, the interchange fee impact on a given variable is low compared to the p or P (AR) part but it exists. The IF regressors have significant standard errors. In all cases, the estimate of the error term variance (denoted by σ^2) is low, greatly contributing to the likelihood of the models.

Table 15 includes the number of goodness of fit measures for estimated models, which were selected from all possible models with

Table 14 The best estimated models

Time series	*Model*	*Coefficients*	
card_acceptors	ARIMA (1,1,0)	ar1 0.8691 (0.1182) σ^2: 2.379 × 10^{-06}	
card_acceptors_with_IF	ARIMA (1,1,0)	ar1 0.8767 (0.1134) σ^2: 2.47 × 10^{-06}	xreg 0.0007 (0.0013)
card_accepting_points_of_sale	SARIMA (1,1,0) (1,0,0)[4]	ar1 0.5679 (0.2502) σ^2: 2.132 × 10^{-06}	sar1 0.6508 (0.2473)
card_accepting_points_of_sale_with_IF	SARIMA (0,1,0) (1,1,0)[4]	sar1 −0.5350 (0.2440) σ^2: 2.101 × 10^{-06}	xreg −0.0014 (0.0015)
payment_terminals	ARIMA (1,1,1)	ar1 0.9894 (0.0220) σ^2: 3.504 × 10^{-06}	ma1 -0.7794 (0.2074)
payment_terminals_with_IF	ARIMA (1,2,0)	ar1 −0.6556 (0.1786) σ^2: 3.442 × 10^{-06}	xreg −0.0047 (0.0046)
number_of_card_payments	SARIMA (0,1,0) (0,1,0)[4]	σ^2: 2.37e−06	
number_of_card_payments_with_IF	SARIMA (0,1,0) (1,1,0)[4]	sar1 −0.6196 (0.2248) σ^2: 1.36 × 10^{-06}	xreg −0.0050 (0.0012)
value_of_card_payments	SARIMA(0,0,0) (1,1,0)[4]	sar1 0.9315 (0.0522) σ^2: 5.246 × 10^{-06}	
value_of_card_payments_with_IF	SARIMA (0,1,0) (0,1,0)[4]	xreg −0.0012 (0.0013) σ^2: 1.731 × 10^{-06}	

Note All the coefficients are statistically significant at least at the siginificance level 0.05. Residual standard deviations denoted by σ^2 are very low (note that they apply to models built on log-transformed and normalised data)
Source Own calculations based on NBP data

Table 15 Models' goodness of fit

Models	*log(L)*	*AIC/AICc*	*BIC*	*MAPE*
card_acceptors	96.07	−188.14/−187.39	−186.25	0.1319
card_acceptors_with_IF	96.23	−186.46/−184.86	−183.63	0.1299
card_accepting_points_of_sale	97.03	−188.06/−186.46	−185.23	0.1156
card_accepting_points_of_sale_with_IF	78.53	−151.07/−148.89	−148.94	0.0920
payment_terminals	92.66	−179.31/−177.71	−176.74	0.1478
payment_terminals_with_IF	88.76	−171.52/−169.80	−168.84	0.1362
number_of_card_payments	76.87	−151.73/−151.42	−151.02	0.0961
number_of_card_payments_with_IF	82.35	−158.71/−156.53	−156.58	0.0801
value_of_card_payments	71.43	−138.85/−137.93	−137.31	0.1716
value_of_card_payments_with_IF	80.35	−156.70/−155.70	−155.29	0.0894

Source Own calculations based on NBP data

predetermined restrictions (see Sect. 3.3.1.1 "Data, Procedure and Assumptions"). They all fit the empirical data well, maximise the log-likelihood, minimise the Akaike and Bayesian Information Criteria. The out-of-sample Mean Absolute Percentage Errors (MAPE) do not exceed 0.2% in any of the models. In line with the principle of parsimony, simpler models are preferred, so even if including more AR or MA parts would increase the likelihood of a model, their inclusion would not be sufficiently justified taking account of the AICs which penalise the number of parameters.

A set of portmanteau tests of residuals were developed to check whether they behave like white noise. All the model pass the Shapiro–Wilk test of normality (Table 16). Except for the value of card payments (without IF) model, the remainder in all other models does not autocorrelate, hence the irregulars are independently distributed. Ljung–Box and Box-Pierce statistics also confirm that the irregulars have no remaining autocorrelations.

The diagnostic checking for residuals can be presented on the example of the payment terminal time series (Fig. 22). In both models (without IF and with IF) Quantile-to-Quantile (Q–Q) plots support the assumption that they are normally distributed. The correlograms and partial correlograms (when the effects of other lags are partialled out) show that at no lag the bound of significance is exceeded. The Ljung–Box and Box–Pierce statistics are well above the limit, indicating non-significance and no remaining autocorrelations.

Table 16 Models' diagnostics

Models	*Shapiro–Wilk test*	*ACF/PACF of residuals*	*Ljung–Box and Box–Pierce statistics*
card_acceptors	S–W=0.94, p-value=0.21	Within limits	No autocorrelation
card_acceptors_with_IF	S–W=0.94, p-value=0.21	Within limits	No autocorrelation
card_accepting_points_of_sale	S–W=0.95, p-value=0.35	Within limits	No autocorrelation
card_accepting_points_of_sale_with_IF	S–W=0.93, p-value=0.17	Within limits	No autocorrelation
payment_terminals	S–W=0.96, p-value=0.51	Within limits	No autocorrelation
payment_terminals_with_IF	S–W=0.97, p-value=0.78	Within limits	No autocorrelation
number_of_card_payments	S–W=0.93, p-value=0.15	Within limits	No autocorrelation
number_of_card_payments_with_IF	S–W=0.95, p-value=0.31	Within limits	No autocorrelation
value_of_card_payments	S–W=0.95, p-value=0.42	Not within limits[a]	Autocorrelation[a]
value_of_card_payments_with_IF	S–W=0.97, p-value=0.75	Within limits	No autocorrelation

Notes [a]lag 6 and lag 7 for ACF of residuals slightly exceed the bound, p-value of Ljung–Box and Box–Pierce statistics is below 0.05
Source Own calculations based on NBP data

3.3.1.4 Application

As the goodness of fit measures reveal, all ten estimated models fit the historical data very accurately. In order to check which models, without or with an interchange fee, perform better, it is worth comparing how they do in forecasting.

According to assumptions, the original dataset was broken down into the initialisation set containing 20 observations (2010–2014) and the holdout set containing 8 more (2015–2016). Their performance in forecasting accuracy is shown on figures below.

Figure 23 presents the entire set of historical data over the period 2010–2016. Both models, the ARIMA card acceptors model with an interchange fee explanatory variable and the model without an additional regressor, develop forecast values close to empirical values. Both models follow almost a linear trend.

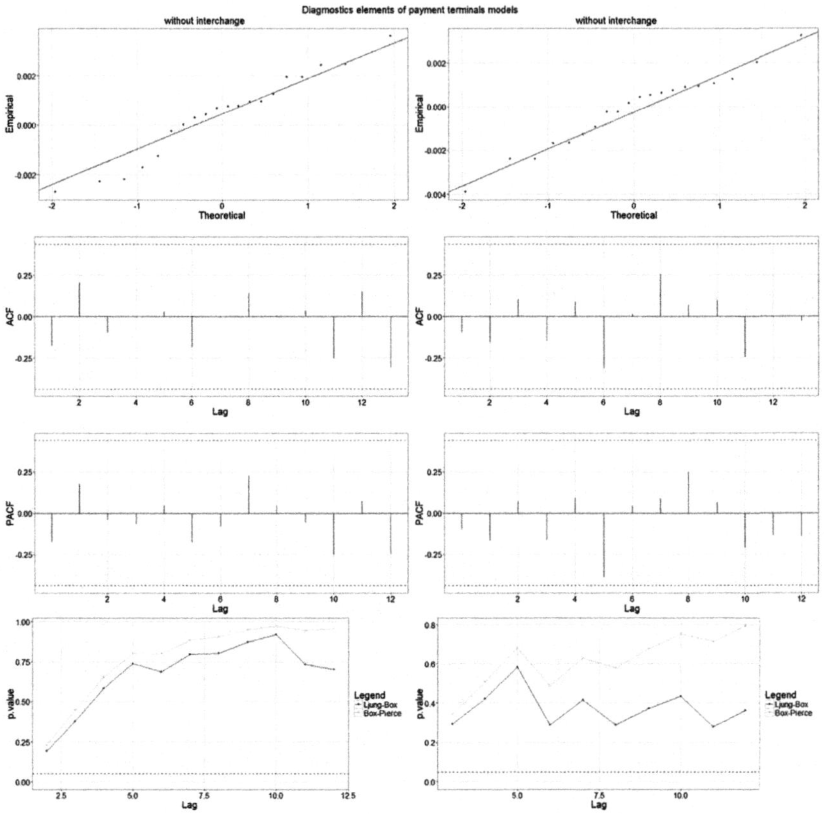

Fig. 22 Diagnostic checking by payment terminals models (without and with the interchange fee as regressor) (*Source* Own calculations based on NBP data)

From Fig. 24 one can see that all four models based on time series representing the card accepting network are forecasting the empirical data with a small error. However, the ARIMA payment terminals with IF model performs particularly well and mimics the actual trend.

Regarding the models exhibiting the card usage, the forecasted values in models with IF stick to the empirical data better. Those predicted by the number of card payments without IF model goes astray (Fig. 25). Judging by the distance from the line of empirical data, the forecast

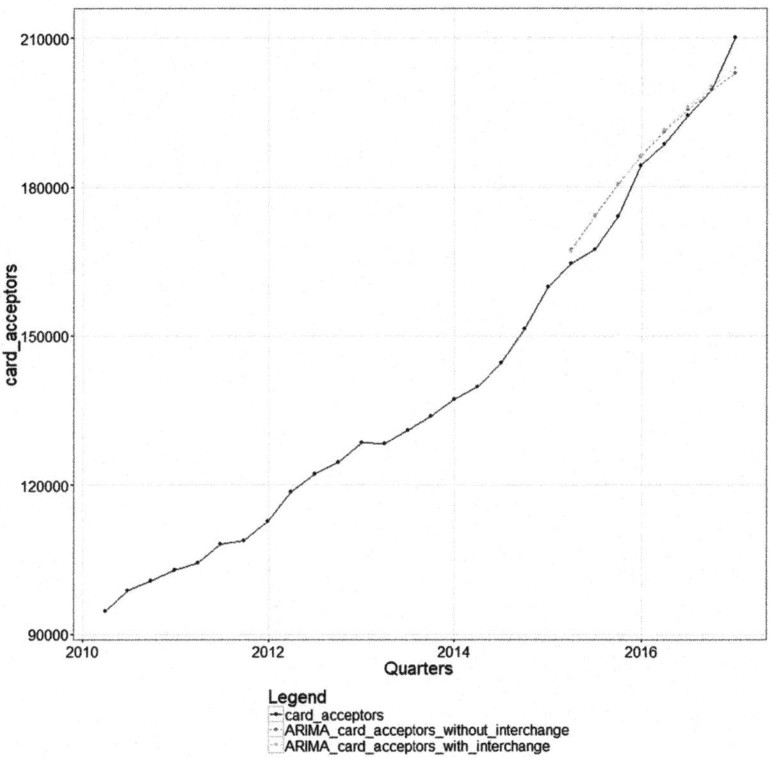

Fig. 23 Forecasting accuracy of card acceptors models (without IF and with IF) against the empirical data in years 2010–2016 (*Source* Own calculations based on NBP data)

accuracy of the value of card payments without IF model could be better (also this model does not confirm the assumption of no autocorrelation of residuals).

Table 17 compares all the estimated models in terms of the MAPE used as an indicator of how much the theoretical values deviate from the empirical distribution of data over the holdout set. With the exception of card accepting points-of-sale without IF model (in this case, the difference between the model without IF and with IF amounts barely to 0.44 percentage point), all models with IF perform better (for card acceptors

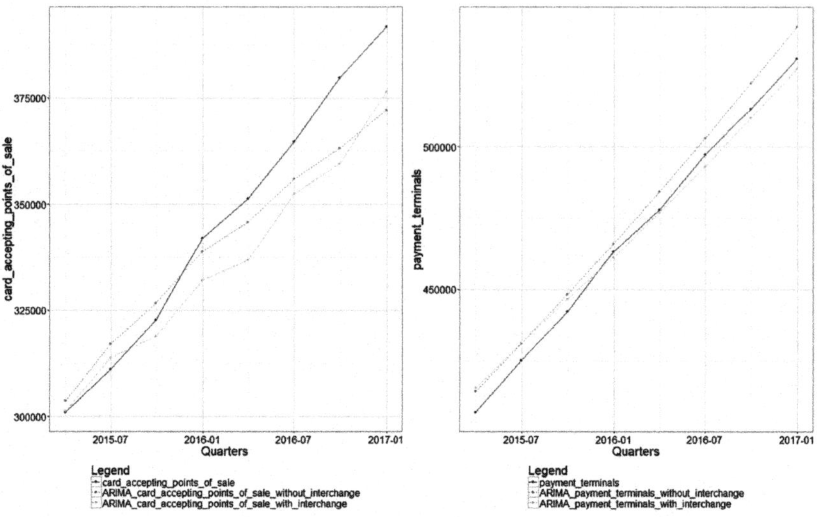

Fig. 24 Performance of card accepting points-of-sale models and payment terminals models in the holdout set over 2015–2016 (*Source* Own calculations based on NBP data)

they are almost the same). Errors are small, even smaller than 1% in the payment terminals with IF model. Thus the evidence is found that the models with IF yield more accurate forecasts and the models without IF lack some essential element. After adding data for 2017 quarters to the testing set and building the models again, the forecasts are developed, for which the difference in the MAPE is even more significant to the advantage of the models with IF.

3.3.2 Findings

The estimated impact of interchange fee reductions on card payments acceptance and card usage in the years 2013–2016 can be measured by comparing two scenarios: the first one, in which it is assumed that the interchange fee remains constant over the entire period at the level from the year 2012 (1.6%); the second one, in which the interchange fee is gradually reduced. In other words, predictions of two models are compared: the one with an IF equal to 1.6% and the second one with a decreasing IF. Calculations are done for intervals when actual

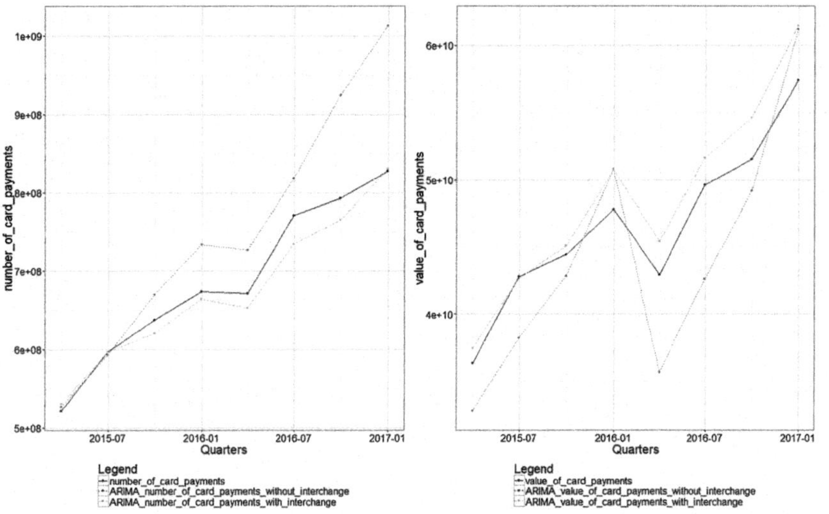

Fig. 25 Performance of models representing card usage in the holdout set over 2015–2016 (*Source* Own calculations based on NBP data)

Table 17 Mean Absolute Percentage Errors of all estimated models' predictions (over the holdout set: 2015–2016)

Models	*MAPE*
card_acceptors	1.99
card_acceptors_with_IF	1.98
card_accepting_points_of_sale	2.28
card_accepting_points_of_sale_with_IF	2.72
payment_terminals	1.43
payment_terminals_with_IF	0.91
number_of_card_payments	8.69
number_of_card_payments_with_IF	2.15
value_of_card_payments	9.04
value_of_card_payments_with_IF	4.23

Source Own calculations based on NBP data

interchange fee rates were in force; however, the assumption about the pass-through effect holds, hence the smoothed time series of the interchange fee (for extended explanation see Sect. 3.3.1.1 "Data, Procedure and Assumptions") are built in the models with a gradually decreasing interchange fee rates.

Overall, the modelled variables were more affected by time-dependent disturbance than by the interchange fee exogenous variable. Although the IF coefficients were much lower than (S)AR coefficients, the change in interchange fees had a meaningful influence on the card payments acceptance network and the card usage in Poland (Table 18). The relationship is inversely proportional, which means that the fall in interchange fees caused the rise in card payments acceptance and in the number and value of card payments.

The summary Table 18 demonstrates the effect of interchange fee decreases compared to a scenario in which an interchange fee would have stayed unchanged at 1.6%:

- the number of points-of-sale accepting card payments was 9 thousand higher (ca 2.5% of all points-of-sale accepting cards as of 2016 Q4[3]),
- the number of payment terminals was 40 thousand higher (ca 8% of all payment terminals as of 2016 Q4),
- the number of card payments was 771 million higher (ca 10% of card payments made between 2013 Q1 and 2016 Q4),
- the value of card payments was PLN 21 billion higher (ca 3% of card payments made between 2013 Q1 and 2016 Q4).

Characteristically, the most meaningful impact of the interchange fee decreases on the card acceptance network happened after the interchange fee was reduced from 1.3 to 0.5% in July 2014. According to the values forecasted by the models, the number of points-of-sale accepting payment cards increased by 4.2 thousand and the number of payment terminals increased by 18 thousand over a merely two-quarter period (Q3 and Q4 2014), which corresponded to almost 50% of the total estimated change brought about by the interchange fee reduction between 2013 Q1 and 2016 Q4. The card payments acceptance network developed rapidly in the last two quarters of 2014 because new small and medium-sized merchants started accepting cards and also the biggest retail chain in Poland did so (about 2.5 thousand stores and 14 thousand payment terminals).

[3]In order to remain methodologically correct, in all four cases it was computed as a ratio to the theoretical value predicted by each model, not to the historical value.

Table 18 Estimated impact of interchange fee reductions on card payments acceptance and card usage in years 2013–2016

Models	*xreg (IF) coefficient*	*Estimated change after IF reduction from 1.6 to 1.3% 2013q1–2014q2*	*Estimated change after IF reduction from 1.3 to 0.5% 2014q3–2014q4*	*Estimated change after IF reduction from 0.5 to 0.2% 2015q1–2016q4*	*Estimated change in total over the entire period 2013q1–2016q4*
card_accepting_points_of_sale_with_IF	−0.0014	1424	4185	3448	9056
payment_terminals_with_IF	−0.0047	5992	18,026	15,991	40,009
number_of_card_payments_with_IF	−0.0050	58,675,820	93,447,150	619,425,745	771,548,715
value_of_card_payments_with_IF	−0.0012	1,688,273941	2,655,743,983	16,645,169,473	20,989,187,396

Note The card acceptors with IF model failed slightly by displaying an inappropriate relationship: +0.0007 coeff(IF), hence this model was not included in the summary table
Source Own calculations based on NBP data

Regarding the card usage (the number and value of card payments), the positive effect of interchange fee reductions was more evenly distributed over time than in the case of the card payments acceptance network (see the summary table). Relatively higher increase in the number of card payments (ca 10%) compared to the increase of card payment acceptance network suggests the existence of the network effect. New payment terminals generated more card payments and the card usage rose also at the points-of-sale which had been accepting cards before the IF reductions.

To recap this section, it has been proven that the regulatory interchange fee reductions in Poland spurred greater card payments acceptance as well as higher card usage in the years 2013–2016. Claims 1 and 2 from area 1 have been positively verified (see Sect. 1.2.5 “Framework for Assessing the Impact of Interchange Fee Regulation”).

3.4 Bank Profits and Cardholder Fees

This section studies how an interchange fee cap introduced in Poland affected the banking sector and bank clients in Poland. According to the theory, when interchange fees decrease, banks may consider raising fees for cardholders, because they face falling interchange fee revenues and typically they want to keep their card business as profitable as it has been to date. However, the pressure on rising fees is mitigated by competition within the banking sector and bank clients’ resistance to worsening terms and fees. Fee increases at banks may go beyond cards, banks may also try to introduce higher account maintenance fees, as revealed, for example, by studies of the US market (Manuszak and Wozniak 2017).

Calculations presented in this section are mainly based on two data sources:

- KNF (Polish Financial Services Authority)—data for banking income,
- NBP (National Bank of Poland)—data for cards.

In addition, the section includes information on pricing of payment services in Poland, obtained from various market sources. NBP collects data on the value of card payments on a quarterly basis. Starting in June 2013, Polish central bank compares, every half a year, fees and commissions in the Polish banking sector. The comparison covers 19–22 Polish banks, for debit card, bank account and other fees on payment services, which together account for more than 90% of the market (the coverage measured by various indicators, such as: share in total assets or share in the number of clients of the banking sector). However, not all of the products in each category (current bank accounts, debit cards etc.) are covered, only selected ones considered by NBP to be representative for a given bank. If data were available, the alternative and more preferred approach would be to include a wider range of cards and current accounts in each bank.

In this study, the NBP data were refined[4] and used for calculating separate statistics for maximum and minimum fees. Polish banks may charge varying fees for the same service, e.g. a monthly fee for a debit card depending on how "transactional" it is, i.e. how intensely it is used. Therefore, if certain conditions are met, such as a certain number or value of payments per month made by a client, the bank may decrease or even fully waive a monthly fee for a debit card or for an account. One of hypotheses tested below by calculating the average maximum and minimum fees (and corresponding statistics) is that the introduction of interchange fee caps induced banks to non-linearly alter the menu of prices for debit cards and current accounts.

3.4.1 Interchange Fee Revenues and Banking Income

The Polish banking sector profitability measured by ROE (return-on-equity) or ROA (return-on-assets) indices tends to be higher than the European average. ROE and ROA ratios are usually computed based on net profit, which means that they may not fully reflect changes in the main income category for banks, i.e. the banking income and its two major components: net interest income and net fee income. Research into the latter income items provides more information about problems affecting banks than an investigation of only net profits and ROE and ROA ratios.

Interchange fees generate for banks revenues included in the fee-based income. According to calculations presented below, in 2012, when a weighted average IF rate was 1.6% in Poland, the interchange fee revenues corresponded to as much as 12.4% of the entire net fee income of

[4]The NBP data on fees and commissions in the Polish banking sector were refined by removing minor inconsistencies and by filling missing data. In order to keep an exact comparability in the sample, i.e. have the same products over the entire period, 19 banks were included for calculations in the final set of data.

the Polish banking sector, whereas in 2016, when the weighted average IF rate dropped to 0.22%, only to roughly 3.5%. It shows that, prior to the reform, IF revenues were relatively more important for banks.

Polish banks do not report interchange fee revenues; IF revenues are seldom revealed in their financial statements. Fortunately, it is possible to estimate these revenues by taking NBP data on value of card payments at physical points-of-sale and multiplying them by adequate IF rates (e.g. 0.2% for debit cards and 0.3% for credit cards since 2015 Q2 onwards). For the existing market setup, actual interchange fee tiers were taken for estimations. The alternative hypothetical scenario assumed that the interchange fee remains constant over the entire period at the level from the year 2012 (1.6%).

The first difference appears in 2013, when the IF rates were not yet decreased by a legislative act but lowered *quasi* voluntarily by payment organisations. Back then, banks earned around PLN 367 million less than they would have if the IF rates had been as high as before. The difference rose to more than PLN 1 billion in 2014, PLN 2.2 billion in 2015 and nearly PLN 2.8 billion in 2016 (Fig. 26). In these three years, two regulatory decreases of interchange fees took place. The overall figure, PLN 6.46 billion, would have been the potential financial gain for the demand side of the market in the years 2013–2016, had the interchange fee reductions been fully passed through to merchants and consumers and had cardholder fees not been increased.

In actual absolute values, interchange fee revenues rose from 2010 to 2011 by PLN 205 million, from 2011 to 2012 by PLN 221 million, but then—along with IF reductions—they were falling in each year: in 2013 by PLN 194 million, in 2014 by PLN 364 million, in 2015 by PLN

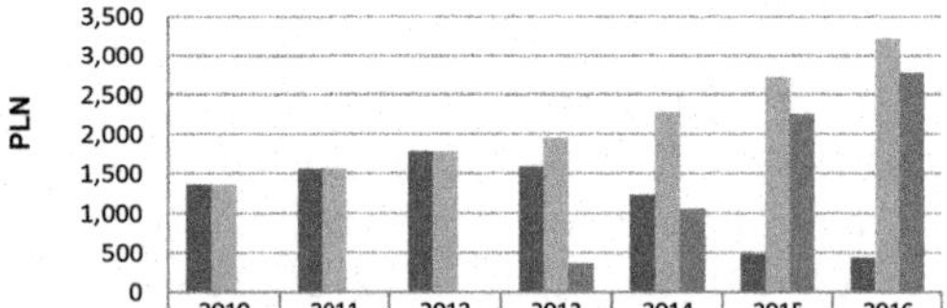

	2010	2011	2012	2013	2014	2015	2016
IF revenues of banks (actual IF rates)	1,356	1,562	1,782	1,588	1,224	476	440
IF revenues of banks (IF rate 1.6%)	1,356	1,562	1,782	1,955	2,279	2,731	3,224
difference	0	0	0	367	1,055	2,255	2,785

Fig. 26 Interchange fee revenues in PLN million (existing market setup vs. simulation) (*Source* Own calculations based on NBP data)

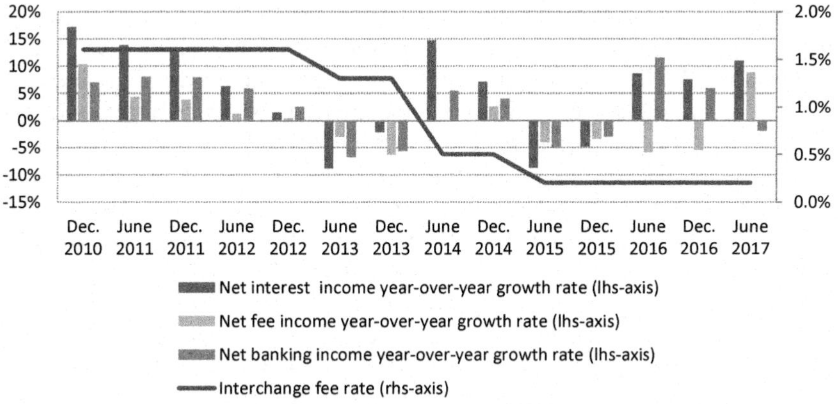

Fig. 27 Net interest, fee and banking income year-over-year growth rates vs. IF rate (*Source* Own calculations based on KNF data)

748 million and in 2016 by PLN 36 million. In total, for the years 2013–2016, banks earned PLN 1.34 billion less on interchange fees. This is the amount they may have attempted to recoup by raising other fees.

The net banking income in Poland (Fig. 27) was affected in the years 2013–2015 by a number of concurrent factors: falling interest rates, rising contributions to the Bank Guarantee Fund (BFG) and—especially in terms of the net fee income—by falling revenues on bancassurance and on interchange fees. A net fee income growth rate in the years 2013–2016 remained negative with the exception of December 2014, when it was slightly positive (year-on-year 2.6% corresponding to PLN 354 million for the entire Polish banking sector along with foreign branches).

A series of central bank's interest rates reductions was a significant challenge for Polish banks in the years 2012–2015. The main refinancing interest rate fell from 4.75% in May 2012 to 1.50% in March 2015, but only in 2013 it dropped by 1.75%, which had a negative effect on the net interest income for the banking sector. In addition, banks had to contribute more to BFG, paying not only a standard annual fee and a fee for the deposit protection fund, but also a new prudential fee (increasing over time), introduced in compliance with the Basel III accord and CRD IV/CRR requirements. The capital gathered from prudential fees paid by banks to BFG was later used to defray the costs of insolvency and restructuring proceedings of some defaulting credit unions and cooperative banks.

Regarding the net fee income, in March 2013 banks started adapting to new guidelines and recommendations of KNF (Polish Financial Supervision Authority) on identification and accounting of bancassurance revenues, which ceased to be treated as one-off fee income attributed to the current period at the time of sale of an insurance policy. The rules became more complex and required banks to divide the revenue into different categories and record it over longer periods. On top of that, IF rates began to fall, with the most significant reduction in 2014: from average 1.3% to uniform 0.5%. Thus, the net fee-based banking income was hit strongly, though it was hit more in 2013 and in 2015, when in the first half-year the second IF reduction to 0.2/0.3% occurred, than in 2014, when in the second half-year banks managed to increase fee-based revenues and the net fee income, as evidenced by aggregated data on banking income and its components (Fig. 27). According to KNF's report on the situation of Polish banks in 2014, this slight increase in the net fee income came as a result of increases in the following items (KNF 2015: 33):

- fees and commissions charged on different bank products and services,
- fees and commissions on bank credits,
- number and value of non-cash transactions (cards and credit transfers),
- fee-based revenues from the capital market.

There is no precise information on the impact of each of the items. The first item comprises, among others, cardholder and accountholder fees. Certainly, they must have been increased. However, in 2014, due to lower interest rates, banks saw a consumer lending growth, which generated not only interest but also fee income. It was another important source of fee-based revenues.

It can be inferred from this initial analysis of the changes in the net fee income that Polish cardholders and accountholders were not seriously impacted by the rising fees. Over the 2013–2016 period, the net fee income fell seven times out of eight, comparing year-on-year growth rates (June-to-June, December-to-December). In absolute values, the net fee income for the Polish banking sector along with foreign branches was PLN 1.74 billion lower in December 2016 than in December 2012 (or PLN 1 billion lower if comparing December 2015 to December 2012 values).

3.4.2 *Pricing of Debit Cards and ATM Cash Withdrawals*

Polish commercial banks issue debit cards under Visa and Mastercard brands as a basic payment instrument. Every bank client opening a current account is offered a debit card. Bank clients use debit cards for withdrawing cash at ATMs and for purchasing goods and services at physical and online shops. The share of non-cash transactions made with payment cards is quickly growing. According to the Polish central bank data as of the end of June 2017, payments at shops accounted for 84% in number and 40% in value of all card transactions (debit and credit cards combined). Debit cards are far more popular than credit and charge cards in Poland. Almost 80% of cards issued in Poland in June 2017 were debit cards and they represented in number more than 91% and in value more than 92% of all card transactions. On average, nearly every (current) accountholder in Poland had at least one debit card in his wallet in 2017.

Polish banks do not charge for issuing a debit card, neither do they charge an annual maintenance fee for a debit card but they can charge such a fee on a monthly basis. Cash withdrawals from the bank's own ATMs are, in principle, free of charge, whereas those from other banks' ATMs domestically and abroad may be subject to a fee.

Already in the third quarter of 2013, when the parliament passed the law amending the Polish act on payment services, it became known on the market that the rate of interchange fee would be limited effectively to 0.5% of the transaction value by 1 July 2014. Banks were well aware of the legislation coming soon in force and they gave a leading response by gradually adjusting terms and fees accordingly. First, they started to withdraw from card rewards. The so-called moneyback programmes or cashback reward programmes incentivising to pay more by card, where a cardholder could have received a certain monetary amount back depending on card spending, began to disappear. Second, banks started to introduce more commonly than before higher but conditional fees. As evidenced from Figs. 28 and 29, banks were adopting to decreasing IF rates already at the end of 2013. However, the increase of an average maximum monthly fee for debit cards amounted to just around PLN 1 (EUR~0.25) over one-and-a-half year period between December 2013 and June 2015, when IF rates were subject to regulatory reductions.

New rules regarding conditional fees had an upside for cardholders. As shown on charts included in Fig. 2, the minimum monthly fee for a debit card fell by 57% in December 2013 and by 4% in June 2014. Also,

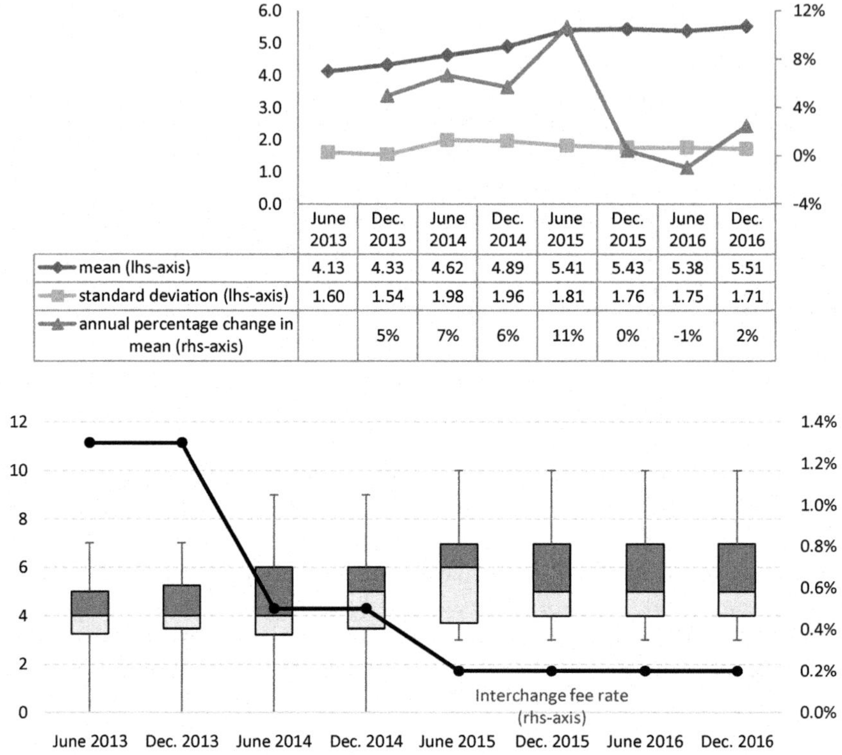

	June 2013	Dec. 2013	June 2014	Dec. 2014	June 2015	Dec. 2015	June 2016	Dec. 2016
mean (lhs-axis)	4.13	4.33	4.62	4.89	5.41	5.43	5.38	5.51
standard deviation (lhs-axis)	1.60	1.54	1.98	1.96	1.81	1.76	1.75	1.71
annual percentage change in mean (rhs-axis)		5%	7%	6%	11%	0%	-1%	2%

Fig. 28 Maximum monthly fee for a debit card (in PLN) (*Source* Own calculations based on NBP data)

the box-and-whisker plots from Fig. 2 clearly illustrate that the minimum monthly fees went down significantly, the Q1 statistic (25th percentile) became as low as nil and the Q3 statistic (75th percentile) stood around 2.5 PLN (~0.6 EUR) in December 2013/June 2014. This translates into a possibility for cardholders to have a monthly debit card fee fully waived, provided they fulfilled given requirements—a minimum card usage in a month.

Regarding card-related services, such as cash withdrawals at ATMs, banks also employed new terms. Overall, the increases of fees as such were low. Polish banks set cash withdrawal fees at other banks' ATMs

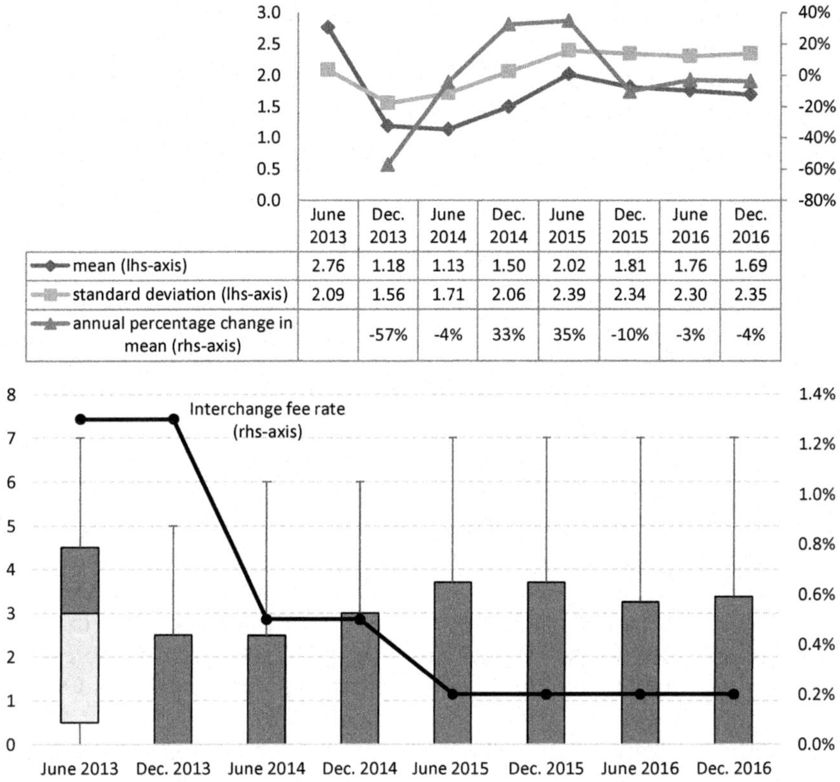

	June 2013	Dec. 2013	June 2014	Dec. 2014	June 2015	Dec. 2015	June 2016	Dec. 2016
mean (lhs-axis)	2.76	1.18	1.13	1.50	2.02	1.81	1.76	1.69
standard deviation (lhs-axis)	2.09	1.56	1.71	2.06	2.39	2.34	2.30	2.35
annual percentage change in mean (rhs-axis)		-57%	-4%	33%	35%	-10%	-3%	-4%

Fig. 29 Minimum monthly fee for a debit card (in PLN) (*Source* Own calculations based on NBP data)

using a mixed formula: there is a minimum fixed fee, not less than e.g. PLN 4 (~EUR 1) and a percentage fee, e.g. 3%. In principle, there were some increases of these fees at Polish banks over December 2013–June 2015 period, especially at the period's beginning, but in reality the median value had hardly changed—with a stable 3% for cash withdrawals at other banks' ATMs domestically and abroad, and PLN 5 or 9 as a minimum fee for domestic and foreign cash withdrawals at other banks' ATMs respectively. However, some banks made other adjustments having a positive effect on their profit and loss account: they introduced various new terms and fees, e.g. restricted the number of free cash withdrawals at other banks' ATMs per month, introduced new fixed fee for unlimited number of cash withdrawals at other banks' ATMs and abroad or a new fee for currency conversion when withdrawing cash abroad. Overall, the effect of these corrections for cardholders can be considered minor.

3.4.3 Pricing of Current Bank Accounts

In recent years the number of current bank accounts in Poland has risen. According to NBP data, as at the end of 2016 there were 41.6 million current bank accounts held by Polish natural persons. Out of 38 million people living in Poland around 70% are 19–70 years old, which means that as of December 2016 an average Pole had no fewer than 1.6 current payment accounts. Nevertheless, in reality, up to 20% of the Polish society had no bank account and used no bank services at all, so effectively those adult Poles who had a relationship with a bank often held two payment accounts or more. An increasing number of Poles use electronic banking, 31 million in total, of which ~14 million were active users in December 2016 (some bank clients using more than one bank may be double counted). At that time, almost 8 million Poles were accessing their bank account from a mobile device (smartphone or tablet). Out of them, 1 million were using the mobile channel only.

The theory implies that there should be more direct correlation between movements in IFs and debit card fees than between movements in IFs and current bank account fees (see Chapter 1). In the latter case, more factors may be at play. This study seems to confirm this rule. Contrary to expectations, and judging only by the results of the study based on NBP data obtained from bank surveys (19 major banks in Poland and 19 representative accounts covered), the average maximum current account fee went up in December 2013 but dropped in June 2014 and in December 2014 (Fig. 30). Throughout 2014, however, the standard deviation was rising. In December 2014, the coefficient of variation became more than 40 percentage points higher than in December 2013 (93.6% vs. 51.4%) meaning that banks were not following the same price strategy.

Just like minimum debit card fees did, minimum current bank account fees fell in advance of the 2014 IF decreases, already in

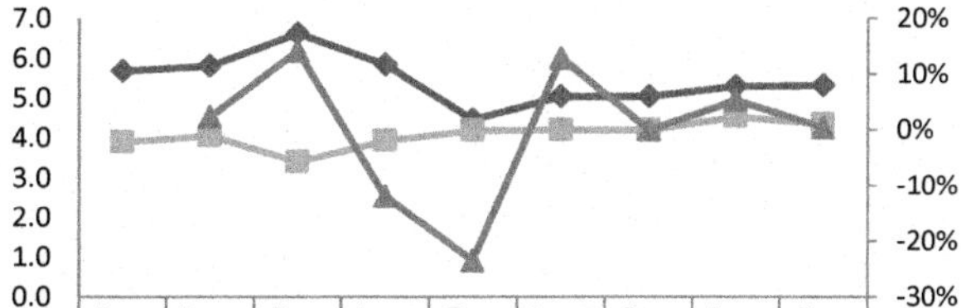

	Dec. 2012	June 2013	Dec. 2013	June 2014	Dec. 2014	June 2015	Dec. 2015	June 2016	Dec. 2016
mean (lhs-axis)	5.67	5.80	6.61	5.82	4.46	5.03	5.03	5.29	5.31
standard deviation (lhs-axis)	3.88	4.05	3.40	3.93	4.17	4.20	4.20	4.52	4.34
annual percentage change in mean (rhs-axis)		2.3%	14.1%	-11.9%	-23.5%	12.9%	0.0%	5.2%	0.3%

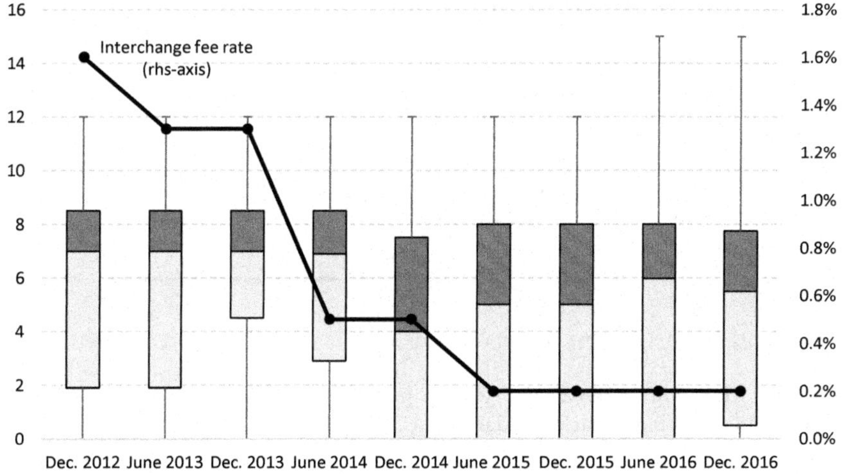

Fig. 30 Maximum monthly fee for a current bank account (in PLN) (*Source* Own calculations based on NBP data)

December 2013. Box-and-whisker plots visualise smaller boxes with lower third quartiles starting in December 2013 (Fig. 31).

Market research (on selected banks' terms and fees tables, executed by the author) and other commercial studies (such as the one commissioned in 2014 by the Union of Entrepreneurs and Employers) confirm that during this turbulent period, when IFs were reduced by regulatory forces, Polish banks altered the terms and fees for current accounts to

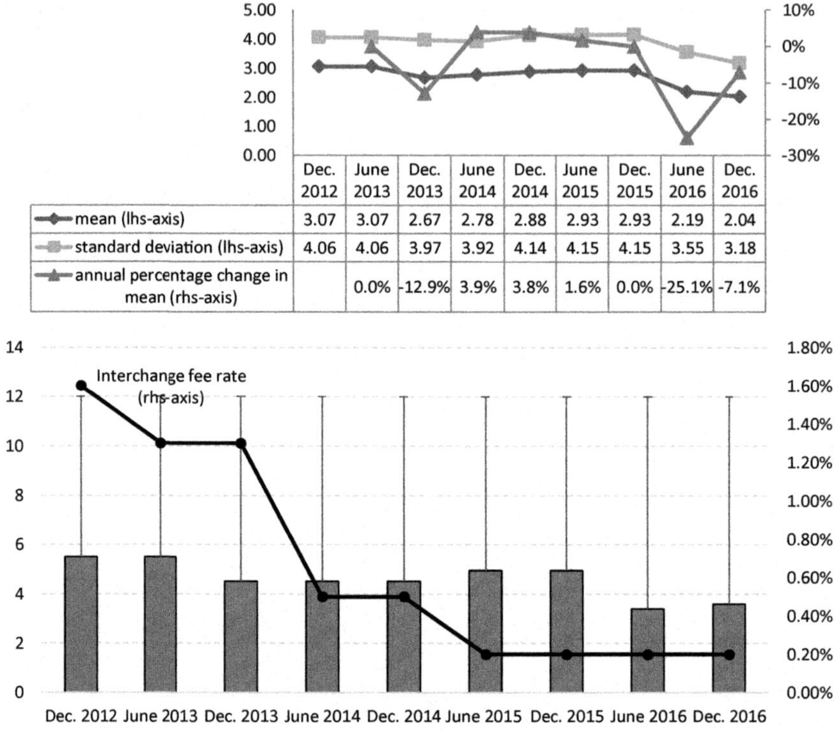

	Dec. 2012	June 2013	Dec. 2013	June 2014	Dec. 2014	June 2015	Dec. 2015	June 2016	Dec. 2016
mean (lhs-axis)	3.07	3.07	2.67	2.78	2.88	2.93	2.93	2.19	2.04
standard deviation (lhs-axis)	4.06	4.06	3.97	3.92	4.14	4.15	4.15	3.55	3.18
annual percentage change in mean (rhs-axis)		0.0%	-12.9%	3.9%	3.8%	1.6%	0.0%	-25.1%	-7.1%

Fig. 31 Minimum monthly fee for a current bank account (in PLN) (*Source* Own calculations based on NBP data)

make it more challenging for clients to avoid paying monthly fees. Clients were frequently obliged to meet certain conditions, such as: securing a required minimum value of funds coming every month to an account or executing a certain number of card payments or keeping the minimum average balance at an account. The portfolio of current bank accounts at Polish banks is diverse. Typically, Polish banks offer a few types of payment accounts for consumers and companies. The menu of fees can differ from one account to another. During the time of IF reductions, banks were modifying their fees accordingly. Even if a monthly fee for the main type of a current bank account barely changed, banks would amend fees on other current account types or sometimes stop offering a given account type to certain client segments and start offering a new one with amended terms and fees.

3.4.4 Findings in a Nutshell

This part presents a concise summary of the interchange fee cap's impact on bank revenues as well as on cardholder and accountholder fees in Poland over the 2013–2016 time span. It has been estimated that the reduced interchange fees lowered bank revenues in this period by ~PLN 6.5 billion (~EUR 1.6 billion). The estimation assumed juxtaposing IF revenues based on real IF rates with a hypothetical scenario where IFs stayed unchanged at 1.6% from 2012 and earlier. The PLN 6.5 billion is a high financial benefit for merchants and consumers in Poland. This amount would be fully paid in merchant fees and prices of goods and services if the interchange fees had not been reduced. In absolute values, interchange fee revenues of banks on card payments executed in brick-and-mortar shops (not including online transactions) fell by PLN 1.34 billion between 2013 and 2016.

Polish banks, however, made attempts not to be in loss and recoup lost IF revenues by:

- introducing nonlinear pricing menu for cards and current bank accounts,
- making it more difficult for cardholders and accountholders to avoid paying a fee for a debit card or a current bank account.

Some of the banks did not react to reductions in interchange fee rates and did not change their pricing for cards and bank accounts at all. Those banks which did so often introduced nonlinear pricing menu, i.e. if certain conditions were not met, such as required minimum number and value of card payments in a month or required minimum average balance on a current bank account, clients needed to pay higher fees. If conditions were met, clients paid no fee or a low fee.

Banks in Poland gave a leading response to decreases in interchange fee rates by adjusting the terms and increasing the fees already in December 2013, soon after the Polish IF regulation had been passed in August 2013. Further adjustments of terms and fees were made over 2014 until June 2015. On the other hand, for some debit cards and for some types of current accounts a new possibility emerged to have the fee fully waived, if a client complied with the new requirements set by banks (e.g. minimum card usage in a month or securing a required minimum money inflow to the account). Polish banks, facing decreasing IF revenues, withdrew from moneyback card reward programmes. From the transparency perspective, it could be considered a positive change, because card payments with an additional cost for cardholders, hidden in merchant service charges, stopped being preferred over other payment instruments.[5] Some banks began to impose new fees on card-related products, e.g. for unlimited number of cash withdrawals at other banks' ATMs and abroad. Terms and fees adjustments, on the other hand, enhanced the rationality of bank clients, who closed unused bank accounts and unused cards.

The competitive industry pressure on bank fees, and clients' resistance to higher fees resulted in the net fee income of the Polish banking sector decreasing by PLN 1.74 billion between December 2012 and December 2016 (or PLN 1 billion lower if comparing December 2012 to December 2015 values). The reduction of the net fee income in this period was caused mainly by the decrease in interchange fees. It can be concluded that, notwithstanding banks' attempts to keep fee-based profits the same as prior to IF reductions, they were not successful in doing so. Even if some fees were successfully increased (in particular for debit cards), all in all, the magnitude of the negative impact of IF reductions on cardholder fees was small (compare claim 4 from area 2 in Chapter 1, section "Framework for Assessing the Impact of Interchange Fee Regulation").

[5] However, in the next years, payment organisations in cooperation with selected issuing banks initiated new reward programmes in Poland. Visa Offers was introduced in 2015 and Mastercard Priceless Specials in 2016. The latter substituted Mastercard Rewards and was extended to include all Mastercard and Maestro cards. Visa Offers rewards cardholders for their Visa card payments with rebates on a range of products at Visa partners in the programme. Mastercard Priceless Specials rewards cardholders with points that can be exchanged for different products at Mastercard partners in the programme.

3.5 Card Scheme Fees, Implications for Innovation, Competition and Security

Payment organisations manage their networks by establishing rules and fees applicable to issuers and acquirers, possibly to other types of members or affiliated non-members (e.g. processors, ATM deployers, service providers, payment facilitators, etc.). Each payment organisation has its own system of governance and code of conduct. In Visa, there are, for example, principal and associate members, in Mastercard principal and affiliate customers. Institutions willing to become part of Visa or Mastercard schemes are charged initial licence (as well as implementation and certification) fees, which vary in scope and cost, e.g. pan-regional licences are more expensive. Rules of payment organisations clearly define rights, liabilities and obligations of all parties. Payment organisation rulebooks are comprehensive, cover in detail all areas, including brand management, security of payments, frauds, dispute resolution, surcharges and rebates, honour-all-cards rules, pricing related to authorisation or clearing and settlement of transactions.

In general, fees charged by payment organisations to issuers and acquirers can be categorised into three groups:

- licencing,
- marketing (comprising development),
- processing.

Marketing fees include funds collected by payment organisations to promote card payments, financial education, innovative payment products, etc. Processing fees are transaction- and value-based (except, in Mastercard scheme, a conditional POS minimum terminal fee charged to acquirers on reported POS terminals). Typically, processing and marketing fees are paid by both issuers and acquirers, but they do not necessarily need to pay exactly the same fees or the same rates. The payment organisation can also charge only a specific group of its members and use funds to back another, or spend it on the intended purpose, this way following its brand strategy and deciding about the distribution of funds. By way of fee shifting from one group of members to another and thus discriminating against certain categories of members, payment organisations are potentially able to circumvent interchange fee regulatory decreases. It could happen if acquirers started paying more and issuers less in their scheme fees.

In the event of a card industry facing interchange fee caps, there is a risk of marketing and processing scheme fee adjustment. Licence fees appear to be the least likely to change, since they are fixed in nature and paid on a one-off basis. On the one hand, interchange fees are directly neutral for the profit and loss account of a payment organisation governing the four-corner system. On the other hand, there exists an indirect relationship. Issuer revenues are interchange-fee dependant. Therefore, falling interchange fee rates may render issuers less willing to issue cards of the payment network in which costs of scheme fees have not decreased but issuer revenues generated by this payment organisation cards did (compare the discussion of the reverse competition in Chapters 1 and 2). Obviously, there are countervailing factors. Mastercard and Visa networks are locked-in on the payments market and characterised by strong network effects arising from high card usage and broad card acceptance (compare Chapter 1). Alternative payment instruments or payment schemes may be non-existent, inferior in their overall characteristics or comparatively little used (low network effects), even if they are cheaper and simpler in handling for banks and other payment players. The new regulatory framework created in Europe by PSD2 (the revised Payment Services Directive), which opens up the banks' infrastructure to third-party providers, has the potential to trigger change by threatening the position of card payments with simple credit transfers.

Leaving licencing fees aside, Visa and Mastercard set domestic, intraregional (for payments between different countries within the Euro Economic Area) and interregional fees (e.g. for payments with cards issued in the US and used in Poland). Levels of processing as well as marketing fees can differ between countries. Some fee rates are fixed and amount-based (e.g. EUR 0.00235), some are percentage-based (e.g. 0.085% = 8.5 bps). There are fees for different categories of transactions, such as: POS, ATM, e-commerce. Some of the fees are flat, some are tiered. An example of the latter is Maestro acquirer volume percentage fee rate of less than EUR 50 million (0.035%), from EUR 50 million to EUR 500 million (0.025%) and more than EUR 500 million (0.02%). This fee structure was valid as of 1 July 2014 (it is not anymore, see below). Fees may decrease with the number or value of transactions, which is rewarding for bigger institutions (e.g. Visa authorisation issuer service fee declining with the value of transactions). Typically, issuers and acquirers pay their processing and marketing fees with a monthly or quarterly frequency (sometimes weekly at Mastercard).

Tiered fees allow issuers and acquirers benefit from economies of scale. Tiered fees can be differently calculated. In the current Mastercard's terminology three types of tiered rates are distinguished: progressive, standard and flat. At Visa progressive tiered rates are called stepped. The most simple rate type is a flat fee. In a progressive (stepped) scale for each tier there is a different rate applicable, but unlike for a standard tiered structure, the total fee is calculated step by step, e.g. if a given fee depends on the number of transactions and there are three tiers in the scale (up to 50,000; 50,000 to 150,000 and more than 150,000 transactions) and there is one rate applicable for each of the tiers (EUR 0.05, EUR 0.03 and EUR 0.01, respectively), then for the assumed number of 200,000 transactions, the total fee would be (50,000 × EUR 0.05) + (100,000 × 0.03) + (50,000 × 0.01) = EUR 6000.

Visa pricing is less complex than Mastercard's. Exploring all the rates and their revisions throughout the entire period studied requires access to all data and a careful analysis. Tracing, sometimes subtle, adjustments in fees alone does not give 100% certainty about their effect for issuers and acquirers. A preferred approach would be to study the fee revisions in connection with the actual cash flows from issuers and acquirers to payment organisations. Obviously, the latter is confidential information, which is not made public by payment organisations. However, according to the law on payment services from 30 August 2013 introducing the interchange fee cap in Poland, four-party schemes are obliged to disclose on their internet websites information about interchange fee rates, as well as about acquiring fee rates.

Therefore, the following discussion of the marketing and processing fees charged in Poland by payment organisations in the years 2014–2016 and later has limitations. However, it is a detailed study aimed at showing selected changes in the card scheme domain that can be linked with the interchange fee reductions or explained by the competition game in the market. The study looks at non-confidential acquiring fees attributable to domestic face-to-face transactions at physical points-of-sale (e-commerce and ATM transaction are excluded or not at the core of the analysis).

In Poland payment organisations charge several marketing fees to acquirers. Visa collects the Market Development Contribution, Mastercard collects three marketing fees for: Innovation for Poland

Fund, Card Payment Promotion Fund, Market Development Fund (Table 19).

Mastercard and Visa revise their pricing periodically by sending pricing bulletins/member letters to their customers/members. From Table 19 one can see that the regulatory interchange fee decrease of 1 July 2014 to 0.5% of the payment amount coincided with the increase of the marketing fees for acquirers. Visa doubled the fee rate for the Market Development Fund from 2.5 to 5 bps of the value of POS transactions. Mastercard increased the fee rate for Innovation for Poland Fund from 2.5 to 6 bps, but effectively the rise was much less significant (or even virtually non-existent), because, pursuant to the new law, Mastercard had to stop collecting funds based on Visa payment volumes. Therefore, Mastercard started collecting the Innovation for Poland (I4P) fee based on reported purchase only for its cards. Note that the I4P was paid not only by acquirers but also by issuers. On 1 July 2014, Mastercard reduced the acquiring fee rate for the Market Development Fund from 10 to 3.5 bps. However, it introduced another fee for the Card Payment Promotion Fund (CPPF) at 8.5 bps. In effect, at the time interchange fee rates were reduced to 0.5%, each payment organisation—Visa and Mastercard—increased their marketing fees collected from acquirers effectively by around 2.5 bps. Table 19 presents also fee rates as of 1 January 2018. In Visa network, they had not changed since 1 July 2014, in Mastercard network they fell throughout this period, e.g. on 1 October 2016 Mastercard lowered the I4P fee from 6 to 4.5 bps and the CPPF fee from 8.5 to 7 bps. Interestingly, it was the moment in time when Visa withdrew rebates for acquiring processing, which was most probably the effect of Visa Inc. acquiring Visa Europe and an attempt to unify the business strategy across regions globally. Before their removal, rebates used to be of the stepped variety and depended on the annual aggregated amount of fees paid to Visa (the more an acquirer paid annually, the higher rebate it could be granted). Market Development Fund (MDF) was lowered by Mastercard in July 2015 and this fee has not changed until 2018 (Table 19).

Apart from marketing fees discussed above, Visa and Mastercard also charge other processing fees. There are two major processing fees in Visa network: acquiring association fee and clearing and settlement processing fee. In Mastercard network, there are more processing fees and their composition has changed in the analysed period (Table 20).

Table 19 Marketing fees for acquirers in Visa and Mastercard networks for Poland

Fee name	*Description and purpose*	*Rate as of 30 June 2014 (%)*	*Rate as of 1 July 2014 (%)*	*Rate as of 1 January 2018 (%)*
Market development contribution (Visa)[a]	Aimed to support the development of the entire market, thus benefitting all parties, among which acquirers and retailers	0.025	0.05	0.05
Innovation for Poland fund (Mastercard)[b]	Charged to support new and innovative projects in the Polish card industry	0.025	0.06	0.045
Card payment promotion fund (Mastercard)[b]	Created to advocate the development of card payment solutions in Poland	–	0.085	0.07
Market development fund (Mastercard)[b]	Used to finance various customer–related activities, focusing on building brand awareness and card activation, increasing purchase volumes, cross-border card usage, and other activities	0.1	0.035	0.015

[a]Calculated as a percentage of acquired Visa POS volume per quarter, min payment €2500, [b]Calculated on reported purchase Mastercard, Maestro and Mastercard Electronic branded domestic volumes; for the Innovation for Poland Fund prior to the interchange fee regulatory decrease on 1 July 2014 calculated on both Mastercard and Visa payment volumes

Source Visa and Mastercard acquiring fee tables

Table 20 Selected domestic POS processing fees for acquirers in Visa and Mastercard networks for Poland

Fee name	*Description*	*Rate as of 1 July 2014*	*Rate as of 1 January 2018*
Acquiring association fee (Visa)	Percentage rate applied on acquired POS value of transactions for: (a) deferred debit and credit cards (b) immediate debit and V Pay	(a) Stepped from 0.0325% to 0.0065% (b) Stepped from 0.0150% to 0.0033% (five tiers)	(a) Flat 0.014% (b) Flat 0.010% (revision on 1 January 2017)
Clearing and settlement processing fee (Visa)	Rate in EUR dependent on the number of transactions	Stepped from €0.0235 to €0.0082 per transaction (five tiers)	Stepped from €0.0150 to €0.0035 per transaction (five tiers, revision on 1 October 2014)
Mastercard and Maestro volume fee (Mastercard)	Percentage rate dependent on the value of transactions	Progressive tiered from 0.045% to 0.020% (four tiers on Mastercard, three tiers on Maestro)	Progressive tiered from 0.070% to 0.023% (two tiers, revision on 1 January 2017)
Minimum volume fee (Mastercard)	Conditional percentage fee dependent on the value of transactions (each acquirer charged if it had not paid the minimum fee of €3000 per quarter)	Progressive tiered from 0.000757% to 0.000252% (six tiers)	–
Minimum terminal fee (Mastercard)	Conditional fixed fee in EUR dependent on the number of terminals (paid only if the total amount of this fee is higher than the sum of the acquiring volume fees and the acquiring reported transaction fees, and Mastercard will only bill for the difference (equal to the minimum terminal fees minus acquiring volume fees and acquiring reported transaction fees)	–	Standard tiered (ten tiers, introduced on 1 January 2017)

(continued)

Table 20 (continued)

Fee name	*Description*	*Rate as of 1 July 2014*	*Rate as of 1 January 2018*
Reported transaction fee (Mastercard)	Rate in EUR dependent on the number of transactions	–	Progressive tiered from €0.00300 to €0.00191 per transaction (four tiers, introduced on 1 January 2017)
Authorisation fee (Mastercard)	Percentage rate on the value of authorised Mastercard payments	–	0.009% (introduced on 1 April 2016)
Clearing fee (Mastercard)	Rate in EUR per transaction dependent on the number of weekly transactions and on the transaction amount	<EUR 5 progressive tiered from €0.0096 to €0.0032 EUR 5–100 progressive tiered from €0.032 to €0.0105 >EUR 100 progressive tiered from €0.048 to €0.0158 (four tiers in each EUR amount interval)	<EUR 5 flat €0.00030 EUR 5–25 flat €0.00125 >EUR25–100 flat €0.005 >EUR 100 flat €0.025 (revision on 1 January 2017)

Source Visa and Mastercard acquiring fee tables

Table 20 shows selected, most important processing fees for domestic payment terminal transactions that Visa and Mastercard charge to their acquirers. Fee tables of payment organisations include many more fee items. In 2014 and 2015 there were only a few adjustments of processing fees, e.g. Visa seemed to slightly lower the burden for acquirers on 1 October 2014 by reducing their stepped rates for clearing and settlement processing fee (Table 20). On the other hand, what cannot be seen in Table 2, Visa increased its minimum quarterly service fee from EUR 2170 to EUR 10,000 and also the system access fee, varying from EUR 0 to EUR 120,000 *per annum* (the upper bound rose from EUR 90,000) and adjusted some other fees of lesser importance. The new pricing was revenue neutral to Visa (Visa Europe at that time). More serious revisions in Mastercard network happened afterwards in 2016 and 2017. On 1 April 2016, Mastercard introduced its percentage authorisation fee. This decision was followed by the introduction of two more fees on 1 January 2017 (reported transaction fee and minimum terminal fee, which replaced the minimum volume fee). Also, from 1 January 2017, Mastercard lowered and simplified its clearing fee to a flat rate in EUR tiered by three steps depending on the transaction amount, and decreased to two the number of tiers for volume fees (arguably, slightly higher rates compared to 2014). Mastercard charges acquirers other fees but they are less significant for acquirer's profit and loss account (e.g. file transmission fee, risk acquirer loss data, preauthorisation fee, connectivity fee, etc.). Visa redesigned its acquiring association fees on 1 January 2017 by changing pricing from stepped to flat rates (below revisions of Visa and Mastercard are reiterated and discussed in the context of competition in the market, i.e. emergence of Blik and Inkart systems). Further revisions of domestic scheme fees for acquirers were announced by payment organisations for 2018 and later (e.g. Visa introducing a new authorisation fee and lowering clearing and settlement fees as of 1 April 2018).

Payment organisations adapt to the changing market conditions domestically and internationally by redefining their business strategy, rules and fees. In 2014 when interchange fees in Poland were high (but about to fall to 0.5%), Mastercard announced its Large Merchant Programme aimed at supporting promotion of their cards. For eligible merchants, i.e. those which fulfilled the criterion regarding the minimum face-to-face card turnover, and that of only Mastercard reported share of transactions, an applicable interchange fee rate would be as low as 0.3%.

The way the programme was designed, only the largest retail chain in Poland (Biedronka) could take advantage of it in 2014. It was the same merchant that, due to excessive merchant fees, had not accepted cards before 1 July 2014. Visa, on their part, decided to apply, from January 2015, cross-border interchange fee rates (0.2/0.3%) to transactions acquired by institutions from abroad. Both decisions influenced policymakers in Poland and contributed to the second regulatory interchange fee decrease in 2015 (see Sect. 3.1 "History of Interchange Fee Reductions in Poland").

When regulatory interchange fee reductions occurred in 2014 and in 2015, Visa ended its programme aimed at supporting card acceptance in rural areas and at small merchants. Mastercard withdrew from financing mPOS terminals (NBP 2015). These decisions might have been, to a certain extent, connected with the interchange fee reductions but they were more probably affected by other factors and by the overall business strategy of Visa and Mastercard. After the regulatory interchange fee decreases, both organisations invested in innovation, e.g. Mastercard used funds collected from marketing fees to support non-bank FinTechs, such as, *inter alia*: uPaid, SkyCash or mPay, which developed electronic wallets (Masterpass) and/or mobile payments for parking fees or public transport tickets. Both organisations invested in their tokenisation services, improving security of card payments and cardholder data by substituting card details with virtual tokens (VTS—Visa Token Service and MDES—Mastercard Digital Enablement Service).

Innovative projects flourished in Poland, giving lie to the opinions that lower interchange fees would make banks and other payment actors spend less on innovation. On the contrary, in the years 2014–2016 banks with their supporting partners built up mobile platforms facilitating proximity NFC (Near Field Communication) payments based on Host Card Emulation (HCE) technology that enabled storing card details in the cloud and not in the SIM card secure element. Thus, issuing banks became fully independent of mobile network operators. At the end of 2016, Android Pay was launched in Poland (now transformed to Google Pay). In parallel, Poles adopted contactless payments widely and the banking sector was modernising the card infrastructure. The progress was quick. In December 2017, around 70% (by number) of all card transactions in brick-and-mortar shops were contactless. The share of contactless payments rose by ca 30 percentage points in three years' time. Poland is one of the leaders in proximity payments in Europe and globally.

The security of card payments in Poland did not suffer from interchange fee decreases. According to NBP data, the share of card frauds in 2014 reported by issuers stood at 0.006% and by acquirers at 0.002% of the card payments value (2015 card fraud rates: issuers 0.005%, acquirers 0.008%, 2016 card fraud rates: issuers 0.005%, acquirers 0.01%). The acquiring fraud rate rose but mainly due to transactions with cards issued outside Poland. Payment service providers implemented 3-D Secure authentication method on a bigger scale, to provide another security layer for Internet payments. Poland had one of the lowest levels of card fraud in Europe (ECB 2015).

Remarkably, with the interchange fee decreases, the competition on the payments market in Poland increased. In late 2013, six large banks in Poland (PKO BP, BZ WBK, mBank, ING Bank, Alior, Millennium) joined forces and founded the Polish Payment Standard as the operator of the mobile payments system Blik. It was licensed in 2014 and went live in February 2015. In subsequent years, this system was supported by more institutions; at the beginning of 2018 already by thirty banks, acquirers and payment integrators. Blik success was built mainly on the quickly growing and convenient e-commerce one-click payments, which gave it an edge over less convenient remote card payments. At physical points-of-sale, Blik was at a disadvantage to card payments, since it was not equipped with the NFC functionality. Blik, although it supports POS payments and ATM cash withdrawals, was promoted as a payment system that does not compete directly with Mastercard and Visa cards in a physical world. It concentrated on mobile P2P instant payments and on e-commerce.

At the time of the interchange fee reductions, KIR (the Polish domestic clearing house) owned by Polish banks began to work on the system for authorising and clearing card transactions that could be regarded as a direct competitor to Visa and Mastercard card processing networks. It became operational in the second half of 2016. Two of the largest banks in Poland—BZ WBK and mBank—signed a contract with KIR then to authorise and clear its card payments and cash ATM transactions. Later on, Inkart system joined also First Data Poland (the second largest acquirer of card payments in Poland) and Euronet and IT Card (the biggest and second-biggest non-bank ATM operators, respectively). However, until 2018, Inkart has not succeeded yet in processing high transaction volumes. One of the reasons for its slower than expected expansion could be the policies of Mastercard and Visa. Both organisations revised their scheme fees accordingly, i.e. lowered some fees, increased or introduced other fees (note that only revisions of acquiring fees for domestic transactions are addressed below).

On 1 January 2017 Mastercard (for rates see Table 20 in this paragraph):

- lowered clearing fee rates (in EUR per transaction), introduced four instead of three amount-based tiers and removed progressive tiered calculation dependent on the weekly number of transactions (translating into clearing fee being independent of the number of transactions processed, which means equal treatment of all acquirers, regardless of their size),
- introduced a new progressive tiered reported transaction fee based on the number of Mastercard transactions (in EUR per transaction),
- increased progressive tiered volume fees (POS Mastercard and POS Maestro) but flattened them to two tiers instead of three (in EUR per transaction),
- introduced a new standard tiered minimum terminal fee (payable only when the sum total of the acquiring volume fees and the acquiring reported fees is lower than the minimum terminal fee dependent on the number of transactions).

Earlier, on 1 April 2016, Mastercard had introduced a new percentage authorisation fee (0.9 bps on domestic Mastercard volumes, since 1 January 2017 the same rate became applicable to intra- and interregional transactions). Visa followed Mastercard and introduced the acquirer authorisation fee as of April 2018. Prior to 1 January 2017, Visa's lower clearing and settlement fee had already been in force since 1 October 2014.

On 1 January 2017 Visa (for rates see Table 20 in this paragraph):

- removed a stepped acquiring association fee and substituted it with a flat rate, linked to quarterly face-to-face Visa gross transaction volumes, lower for debit and V Pay cards and a bit higher for deferred and credit cards,
- introduced a number of changes to domestic and international MOTO, ecommerce and ATM transactions.

In particular, Mastercard's fee revisions could be treated as closely related to the commercial roll-out of Inkart, because Mastercard cut its clearing fees and introduced a new fee on reported Mastercard transactions. This fee would be applicable also to Mastercard's card transactions processed through the system of Inkart, making the latter less price competitive for issuing banks. The 2016–2017 revisions of Mastercard and Visa scheme fees reflected not only the industry organisation in Poland but also the legal framework. Article 7 of the EU Interchange Fee Regulation 2015/571 required separating scheme from processing activities.

The pricing policy of Visa and Mastercard took account of the risk of bringing down the interchange fee rate on debit cards to null in Poland. The risk arose in 2016, when the Polish government considered to step in on the card payments market with the next regulatory intervention capping interchange fees and began to prepare a legislative package. In addition, Polish policymakers expected banks to establish a new domestic card scheme to compete with Visa and Mastercard. Banks were reluctant to do so, having already set up Blik mobile payment system. Amid the threat of further interchange fee decreases in Poland, a few decisions have been made by the commercial card sector in Poland.

The Polish Bank Association (ZBP), Visa and Mastercard signed a letter of intent with the Ministry of Development, in which they committed to support the promotion of cashless payments, digitalisation and card acceptance. They created the Card Acceptance Development Programme aimed at doubling the number of payment terminals in the Polish private sector, a globally exceptional project (although not the only one, Mexico and India initiated actions with similar objectives). Starting from January 2018, every non-card accepting merchant taking part in the Polish Programme, upon meeting simple transaction and information conditions, has the right to instal up to three payment terminals and accept card payments at no cost for a year (merchant fees and rental costs of the terminal fully reimbursed). The Programme is managed by the newly established Foundation Cashless Poland, which intends to collect PLN 600 million over a four-year period. The Programme is financed by:

- payment organisations (PLN 0.015 on each face-to-face debit card transaction),
- banks (PLN 0.01 on each face-to-face debit card transaction),
- acquirers (1 bps on face-to-face debit card turnover).

These bank and acquirer fees are paid on top of scheme fees.

Visa and Mastercard backed also another initiative, launched formally in April 2017 and aimed at popularising cashless payments at the offices of public authorities. The project was at the start managed by the Ministry of Development in cooperation with KIR clearing house, but in 2018 it was transferred under the management of the Foundation Cashless Poland. Payment organisations decreased interchange fee rates to 0.01% (maximum PLN 0.01) on each card-present transaction for public administration offices at POS terminals, but this covers only a fraction of card payments at public administration (not covered are other government payments or. e.g. payments at courts or to the police).

Information retrieved from the official website of SIX Payment Services[6] (acquired by Worldline in May 2018), one of the European acquirers operating also in Poland, reveals the 2017 indicative estimate for the aggregate level of scheme fees paid by Polish acquirers to Mastercard and Visa for domestic general face-to-face purchase transactions (both amount-based and percentage scheme fees included). It turns out, taking into account dozens of fee items, that the aggregate cost of domestic transactions for an acquirer translated into a percentage rate relative to the average transaction value stood at 0.2378% for Mastercard and at 0.1253% for Visa in 2017. This rate could vary between acquirers. Mastercard is a more expensive payment organisation than Visa for acquirers in Poland. In principle, Mastercard is also more expensive than Visa for Polish issuers. However, according to statistics published by the Polish central bank, in December 2017 Mastercard accounted for 44% cards issued and Visa for 55%, whereas in December 2008 Mastercard's market share was only 30% and Visa's 67%. Apparently Mastercard's strategy, including redistribution of funds and rebates for issuers, has been more effective than Visa's in the last decade (reflected by the 14 percentage points increase of Mastercard's share in the number of issued cards).

It seems that the aggregate cost of scheme fees for acquirers proportionate to the card turnover has not changed much in the last couple of years, although payment organisations adjusted scheme fees. The 2014–2015 regulatory interchange fee reductions coincided with revisions and a slight increase of marketing fees at Visa and Mastercard. However, Visa lowered their clearing and settlement fees and introduced issuing

[6]https://www.six-payment-services.com/dam/classic/downloads/scheme-fees/Scheme-Fees-Poland.pdf, 28 December 2017.

and acquiring rebates in 2014. At that time, Mastercard was more passive in changing its processing fees. More profound pricing revisions of Mastercard and Visa scheme fees happened later, in 2016 and 2017. Note, however, that in absolute values Mastercard and Visa profits on domestic card payments in Poland must have been increasing steadily year after year since 2014, because the number and value of card transactions have grown. A study on actual cash flows generated by scheme fees would provide valuable information on that matter.

In conclusion, interchange fee caps in Poland impacted the policy of payment organisations. They reacted directly, e.g. Mastercard introduced its Large Merchant Programme and Visa enabled merchants to benefit from 0.2/0.3% lower rates by changing its rules on cross-border acquiring. Afterwards, when the card industry faced the threat of zero interchange fee for debit cards in Poland, payment organisations set interchange fees for payments at the public administration offices at a very low level (maximum PLN 0.01), and, together with the Polish Bank Association, issuers and acquirers, established the Card Acceptance Development Programme. The impact of the interchange fee caps on adjustments of scheme fees was rather indirect. Plausibly, lower interchange fees motivated banks to set up Blik mobile payment system and KIR to build Inkart card authorisation and clearing system. In turn, these decisions impacted strategy of Mastercard and Visa. They adjusted their scheme fees, lowered or redesigned some processing fees, introduced other types of fees (e.g. reported transaction fee at Mastercard, authorisation fee at Mastercard and Visa). Formula of some fees became simpler (fewer steps, more flat rates). Claim 5 from area 3 of the framework for assessing impact of the interchange fee regulations (see Chapter 1) has been confirmed. In general, it seems that the aggregate level of domestic scheme fees has not changed much but adjustments were made in the structure of scheme fees. Security of payments has not suffered. Competition in the Polish payments market has risen as well as innovation.

3.6 Pass-Through Effect in the Holistic Perspective

According to the framework developed in Chapter 1, it is possible to look at the interchange fee regulatory caps from a multitude of perspectives pointing to positives and negatives of the reform. Evaluation consists in estimating the benefits and costs of all parties in the four-corner model and examining different aspects: network effects, competition, innovation, etc. The pass-through takes place in two transmission channels: acquirer → merchant → consumer, and issuer → consumer. Its effectiveness depends on the competition between issuers, acquirers and merchants, on asymmetry of information and on bargaining powers of merchants and consumers. The pass-through of lower interchange fees manifests itself in transmitting the financial savings and in creating stronger network effects. The latter are the main benefit of payment instruments. The theory of two-sided markets stresses the importance of network effects.

Section 3.3 found that reductions in interchange fees positively impacted card payments network and card usage in Poland. The analysis confirmed claims 1 and 2 from area 1 of the framework for assessing the impact of the interchange fee regulation (see Chapter 1). Although econometric modelling demonstrated strong autoregressive relationship in all modelled time series, it also proved that econometric models with the interchange fee rate as an explanatory variable were statistically significant and yielded more accurate forecasts, better fitted to the empirical values in the holdout set of historical data. The change in interchange fees had a visible impact, because it induced more merchants to start accepting cards. According to the results of SARIMA modelling, thanks to the reduction of the interchange fee rates alone (excluding impact of other factors) around 9000 new companies joined the card acceptance network and 40 thousand new payment terminals were installed between 2013 Q1 and 2016 Q4. Apparently, for many merchants costs of accepting cards ceased to be detached from the limits of their price elasticity (ceased to constitute a cos barrier). Also, card usage benefitted from interchange fee caps. In the four-year period, the number and value of card payments at physical points-of-sale (excluding remote payments) grew faster, contributing to additional 771 million and PLN 21 billion, respectively. These results suggest that stronger network effects arose in both: new and old locations accepting cards. It seems that a broader card acceptance base encouraged consumers to generally pay more by card after the interchange fee reductions. Future research can be extended to study this aspect in more detail.

Surcharging has never been popular in brick-and-mortar shops in Poland. More popular were rebates for paying in cash and also influencing consumer choice of payment method by limiting the usage of cards for low-value payments. Typically, consumers were facing notices at the counter informing that below a specific amount (PLN 10–20) only cash payment was possible. Merchants were thus prohibiting card payments despite breaking payment organisation rules, since for low-value payments MSCs were likely to eat up merchant's entire profit margin. According to the anecdotal evidence, decreases of interchange fees put an end to such restrictions on card payments.

Section 3.2 explored two merchant surveys from 2013 and 2014/2015 shedding more light on the financial dimension of the pass-through effect from acquirers to small and medium-sized merchants. Large merchants, such as supermarket retail chains or petrol station chains, were not covered by the surveys. However, they benefitted almost instantly from the interchange fee caps due to IF+ and IF++ structures of their MSCs embedded in the contracts with acquirers. According to the 2014/2015 merchant survey, the awareness of the regulation among small and medium-sized enterprises (SMEs) accepting cards in 2014 was not particularly high. 50% of card acceptors knew about the legislation capping interchange fees from 1 July 2014. Around 34% of SMEs declared experiencing decreases in their merchant fees within eight months from the regulatory reduction in interchange fees. On average, their MSCs were cut in half. Even though, 2/3 of small and medium-sized merchants did not take advantage of lower interchange fees, which implies that acquirers benefitted in the short term from asymmetry of information and managed to keep higher margins. On the other hand, the competition between acquirers intensified, because the rate of merchants that swapped acquirers in their card accepting history rose by 3 percentage points from 21 to 24% throughout the year between two editions of the survey. Besides, the 2014/2015 survey shows that acquirers, being afraid of losing merchants to competition, offered better financial terms to a number of SMEs (ca 2/3 of the group which experienced reductions in MSCs, that is of the group constituting around 1/3 of card accepting SMEs at that time). It seems likely that in the next months acquirers passed more savings to merchants. Besides, the SMEs awareness of pricing adjustments on the card payments market must have been increasing steadily (as it had grown between 2013 and 2014/2015 by 7 percentage points from 43 to 50%).

Section 3.4 investigated the adjustments to lower interchange fees in the issuer→consumer (cardholder and accountholder) transmission channel. Banks' interchange fee revenues from card transactions at brick-and-mortar shops fell by PLN 1.34 billion between 2013 and

2016. Due to the growing value of card payments, banks managed to offset a part of lost interchange fee revenues. If interchange fee rates had stayed unchanged at the level from 2012 (1.6%), then banks would have earned PLN 6.46 billion more (by actual value of card transactions 2013–2016). Banks made attempts to recoup lost interchange fee revenues by increasing some fees and by introducing nonlinear pricing menu for cards and current banks accounts. If bank clients were successful in meeting certain conditions, e.g. executed a required minimum number and value of card payments, they paid low or no fees. Otherwise they were charged a monthly fee. This mechanism became more common after the reduction in interchange fees, but not all banks revised their terms and fees in the same way. As evidenced by calculations based on NBP data, the increase of the average maximum monthly fee for a debit card amounted to around PLN 1 (EUR~0.25) between December 2013 and June 2015. Over this one-and-a-half year period, the average maximum monthly fee for a current account went down by PLN 1.6 (EUR~0.4). Average minimum monthly fees for debit cards and current bank accounts went slightly up. Some fees for card-related services were introduced or increased (e.g. for ATM cash withdrawals) and moneyback reward programmes were withdrawn. A number of banks made a leading response to the 2014 interchange fee reduction already in the second half of 2013.

However, due to the competition within the banking sector, the magnitude of negative change for consumers resulting from the interchange fee caps was limited. Between December 2012 and December 2016, the net fee banking income fell by PLN 1.74 billion and the bank fee revenues decreased by PLN 1.76 billion, meaning that bank clients benefitted. In 2014 alone, banks managed to increase their fee-based revenues by PLN 241 million and the net fee income by PLN 354 million, implying that they compensated for a fraction of the interchange fee revenues lost due to the regulatory interchange fee reduction to 0.5% in July 2014. Banks were not successful in compensating for the second interchange fee reduction to 0.2/0.3% in 2015, which harmed their profit and loss accounts even more (IF revenues in 2015 fell by PLN 748 million, fee-based revenues by PLN 853 million and the net fee income by PLN 472 million). As for 2014, banks optimised their fee-based and operating costs. According to the KNF (Polish Financial Supervision Authority), the rise of bank fee-based revenues and the bank fee income in 2014 was not only the effect of the increased fees for debit cards, bank accounts, credit transfers and other bank products and services, but also the result of higher revenues from fees and commissions on consumption bank lending that intensified due to lower interest rates, and of fee-based revenues from the capital market (KNF 2015). Claim 4 from area 1 of the framework for assessing impact of the interchange fee regulations (Chapter 1) was confirmed but as the result of the competition within the banking sector and bank clients' resistance to higher fees, Polish banks were able to recoup only a relatively small part of the lost interchange fee revenues.

Section 3.5 explored how the payment organisations coped with lowered interchange fees, i.e. whether their pricing policy changed or interchange fee decreases were treated neutrally by Visa and Mastercard (the history of interchange fee reductions was presented in Sect. 3.1). Moreover, this part examined whether lower interchange fees incentivised issuers and acquirers to innovate, improve their existing payment services and develop new payment methods. The analysis led to the conclusion that the impact of interchange fee caps on the scheme fees and the strategy of payment organisations was more indirect in nature; a stronger indirect feedback has been detected. Lower interchange fees contributed to the decisions of Polish banks to establish Blik mobile payment system and to the decision of KIR (the clearing house owned by Polish banks) to build a new card processing system, rivalling those of Mastercard and Visa. The competition and innovation on the payments market increased. Contactless and mobile payments boomed. Payment organisations took action in response to new payment systems and adjusted scheme fees, reorganised the rates, structure of fees, introduced new fees to appropriately position themselves towards new competing systems. Of course, Visa and Mastercard took account of falling interchange fee rates also directly, e.g. by increasing marketing fees for acquirers in 2014. However, no hard evidence for major changes in the aggregate level of scheme fees charged to acquirers was found (see claim 5 from area 3 of the framework for assessing impact of the interchange fee regulations in Chapter 1). Based on acquirers' data, the average acquiring cost of scheme fees for face-to-face card transactions in 2017 was higher for Mastercard (0.2378%) than for Visa (0.1253%).

Faced with a threat of the zero cap on interchange fees on debit cards for domestic payments in Poland, Visa and Mastercard decreased interchange fees for payments at public administration offices (part of public government payments) to a negligible maximum rate of PLN 0.01

and, in addition, together with Polish Bank Association, they committed, in the letter of intent signed with the Polish government, to create the Card Acceptance Development Programme. According to the agreement, the Programme is financed by payment organisations, issuers and acquirers. The latter two groups pay for the fund in fees to card organisations charged on top of scheme fees. In the four-year period, the fund managed by the newly established Foundation Cashless Poland is planning to collect PLN 600 million. The ambition of the Programme founders is to double the card acceptance network, i.e. to instal 500–600 thousand new payment terminals in Poland between 2018 and 2021. Each merchant enrolled in the Programme will have all of its fixed and variable acceptance card costs reimbursed for 12 months.

In the chapter, until now, claim 3 from area 1 of the framework for assessing impact of the interchange fee regulation (see Chapter 1) has not yet been approached either quantitatively or qualitatively. The issue whether savings resulting from lower interchange fees and, subsequently, lower merchant fees were passed on in the form of lower prices to consumers is particularly difficult to be assessed. Of key importance in this evaluation is the pace at which reductions in interchange fees are passed through by acquirers to merchants and, then, by merchants to consumers. The two merchant surveys conducted in 2013 and 2014/2015 made clear that the transmission from acquirers to SMEs is not instant, it takes time, even if the competition within the acquiring sector is rising. Large merchants, however, can quickly benefit from lower interchange fees, because their contract provisions with acquirers usually stipulate MSCs in the form of IF+/IF++ or, alternatively, large merchants are better informed and they can promptly renegotiate the financial terms or move to another acquirer with a better offer.

In its initial impact assessment study of the interchange fee reductions in Poland (NBP 2015), Polish central bank estimated, based on questionnaires sent to acquiring institutions, that 60–80% of all card payments were made at points-of-sale of large merchants subject to transparent IF+/IF++MSC structures. It implies that those merchants benefitted instantaneously from lower interchange fees. However, most of these merchants did not declare in the central bank's questionnaire to have passed through the interchange fee reductions in the form of lower prices to consumers. Instead, they acknowledged that savings were invested in improving service, in loyalty programmes or chain development.

2013–2016 was a period of deflation in Poland. According to the Polish Statistical Office (GUS), in 2013 the prices measured by consumer price index (CPI) went up by merely 0.9%, in 2014 there was no inflation, in 2015 prices went down by 0.9% and in 2016 by 0.6%. The contribution of interchange fees in the price setting process cannot be considered significant. Most probably, prices went down due to other factors. However, it seems likely that the reductions in interchange fees slowed down price increases that would have otherwise occurred. Such is also the conclusion from the study of the Reserve Bank of Australia reviewing the interchange fee reform impact in Australia. When CPI is rising or falling at a slow rate (1–2%), it is difficult to isolate the effect of the interchange fee reductions. However, RBA estimated that, ceteris paribus, the savings would likely lead to the CPI being around 0.1–0.2 percentage points lower over the longer term that in the alternative scenario, in which interchange fee rates would remain unchanged (RBA 2008: 25). It would be against the economic theory to assume that changes in business costs are not reflected in prices of goods and services sold by merchants. On the other hand, this is a valid question for further research, how changes in business costs affect business margins and, then, prices.

Based on the reasoning presented and in the absence of concrete evidence contradicting the economic theory, there are no grounds to argue that in the longer term lower interchange fees in Poland were reflected in lower prices, but the short-term dynamics suggests that savings were passed on from acquirers to merchants, and from merchants to consumers with some delay (see claim 3 from area 1 of the framework for assessing the impact of interchange fee regulation in Chapter 1). It seems justified to state that it must have taken up to several years to pass-through to consumers all of PLN 1.34 billion, which is how much less issuing banks raised in interchange fee revenues generated by card transactions at brick-and-mortar shops in the years 2013–2016. Large merchants with IF+/IF++ structures benefitted instantly, but, on average, small and medium-sized merchants waited longer to experience the positive change. Even though price competition is high in Poland, in particular between large retail chains, the consumers did not experience direct financial gains in lower prices of goods instantly but they most likely benefitted from lower price increases over longer time horizon. It needs to be emphasised that merchants and consumers together realised opportunity gains in the years 2013–2016 stemming from lower interchange fees. Otherwise, merchants would have to pay additional PLN 6.46 billion in transaction fees. Obviously, this amount would be included in the prices of goods charged to consumers.

Bibliography

Box G., Jenkins G. (1970) *Time Series Analysis: Forecasting and Control*, San Francisco, Holden-Day.

Box G., Jenkins G., Reinsel G. (1994) *Time Series Analysis: Forecasting and Control*, 3rd ed., Englewood Cliffs, NJ, Prentice-Hall.

Byrski J. (2014) *Nowelizacja ustawy o usługach płatniczych dotycząca opłaty interchange—komentarz praktyczny* (title in English: *Amendment of the Payment Services Act Regarding the Interchange Fee—Practical Commentary*), FROB, BCC, Warsaw.

Byrski J., Marcinkowska A. (2015) *Nowelizacja ustawy o usługach płatniczych z dnia 28 listopada 2014 r. dotycząca opłaty interchange—komentarz praktyczny* (title in English: *Amendment of the Payment Services Act from 28 November 2014 Regarding the Interchange Fee—Practical Commentary*), FROB, BCC, Cracau.

European Central Bank (ECB) (2015) *Fourth Public Report on Card Fraud*, Frankfurt am Main.

Górka J. (2012) *Badanie kosztów akceptacji gotówki i kart płatniczych wśród polskich przedsiębiorców* (title in English: *Study of Cash and Cards Payment Acceptance Costs Among Polish Merchants*), Report in the Research Project of FROB, NBP and FoM UW.

Górka J. (2013) *Efektywność instrumentów płatniczych w Polsce* (title in English: *Efficiency of Payment Instruments in Poland*), Publishing House of the Faculty of Management, University of Warsaw.

Harasim J. (2013) *Interchange Fee and the Competition in the Payment Card Market in Poland,* "Research Papers of Wroclaw University of Economics", No. 316, pp. 55–66.

Interchange Fee Regulation (EU) 2015/751 of the European Parliament and of the Council of 29 April 2015 on Interchange Fees for Card-Based Payment Transactions, OJ EU L 123/1.

Ipsos (2014) (2015) *Badanie obrotu kartowego wśród przedsiębiorców w Polsce* (title in English: *Surveys of Polish Merchants on Card Payments*), Two Editions, Reports, Warsaw.

Komisja Nadzoru Finansowego (KNF, Polish Financial Supervision Authority) (2015) *Raport o sytuacji banków w 2014 r.* (title in English: *Report on the Banking Sector Condition in 2014*), Report, Warsaw.

Maciejewski K. (2013) *Znaczenie opłaty interchange dla rozwoju rynku kart płatniczych w Polsce* (title in English: *Interchange Fee Signifance for the Card Payment Market Development in Poland*), "Copernican Journal of Finance & Accounting", Vol. 2, No. 2, pp. 111–124.

Makridakis S., Wheelwright S., Hyndman R. (1998) *Forecasting: Methods and Applications*, 3rd ed., Wiley.

Manuszak M., Wozniak K. (2017) *The Impact of Price Controls in Two-Sided Markets: Evidence from US Debit Card Interchange Fee Regulation*, "Finance and Economics Discussion Series 2017-074", Washington, Board of Governors of the Federal Reserve System.

Narodowy Bank Polski (NBP) (2012) *Analysis of the Functioning of the Interchange Fee in Cashless Transactions on the Polish Market*, NBP Report, Warsaw.

Narodowy Bank Polski (NBP) (2015) *Analiza skutków obniżenia opłaty interchange w Polsce* (title in English: *Analysis of the Interchange Fee Reductions' Effects in Poland*), NBP Report, Warsaw.

Payment Services Directive (EU) 2015/2366 of the European Parliament and of the Council of 25 November 2015 on Payment Services in the Internal Market (PSD2), OJ EU L 337/35.

Polasik M. (2015) *Stan i potencjał rozwoju sieci akceptacji kart płatniczych w Polsce* (title in English: *Status and Development Potential of the Card Payment Acceptance Network in Poland*), "Acta Universitatis Nicolai Copernici", No. 1, pp. 23–58.

Reserve Bank of Australia (RBA) (2008) *Reform of Australia's Payment System, Preliminary Conclusions of the 2007/08 Review*, April.

CHAPTER 4

Final Remarks

The famous line from Hamlet's soliloquy echoes in its paraphrased form in the card payments industry: *to regulate, or not to regulate?* That is the question. There are many interpretations of Hamlet's dilemma. But what does it mean in the context of interchange fee economics? Does regulation cure the card and payments market from market failure or rather kills it by limiting card organisations' and banks' freedom to run their business at their own discretion? Is it better to stay passive and believe in the invisible hand of the market or be active and navigate towards the optimum, an equilibrium in which joint welfare of consumers and merchants is maximised?

There is no simple answer to that. However, this study based on a careful inspection of the impact of interchange fee reforms in various countries may deliver some useful information. Capping interchange fees and intervening directly in the four-party card schemes' market by lifting restrictions limiting competition on the payment market is a global trend. European, Australian and Asian regulators tend to be stricter than regulators from the USA, Canada and Mexico (see the cases studied in Chapter 2). Ceiling limits on interchange fee rates are set lower outside America, especially in the European Union (0.2/0.3% caps for debit and credit card payments, respectively in the 2015 EU Interchange Fee Regulation covering all member states). It is a globally recognised fact that public authorities oppose the reasoning of four-party card schemes and issuing banks, and see market failure in the card payment market, where the latter two operate.

J. Górka, *Interchange Fee Economics*,
https://doi.org/10.1007/978-3-030-03041-4_4

Contrary to the claims of Visa, Mastercard, banks and to numerous reports and academic studies, many of which sponsored by card organisations, viability of the card system has not been harmed. Cards have continued their vigorous growths after interchange fee reforms, and their share in non-cash transactions has increased, which is clear evidence of the growing role of cards overall. Cards are the most popular cashless payment instrument in the world. One could even challenge the prevailing logic of the detractors of regulation and start wondering whether the interchange fee reforms may have contributed to the thriving of card systems.

The studies conducted in this book may well serve as guidance in this respect. An assessment of the impact of interchange fee regulation in Australia, USA, Spain and Poland, according to the framework developed in Chapter 1, makes the effects apparent. Below, some of the conclusions from the analysis of country cases will be reiterated, but for more details see the summary sections in Chapters 2 and 3 (Sect. 2.2.4 "Summary Comparison and Impact Assessment" and Sect. 3.6 "Pass-Through Effect in the Holistic Perspective").

Strong evidence has been found for claims 1 and 2 from area 1 of the framework for assessing the impact of interchange fee regulation in Europe: Spain, Poland, Italy. Before interchange fees were reduced, their high rates and, more specifically, high merchant service charges, had constituted a serious barrier, especially for small merchants, to accepting cards. Even if the four-corner card model, making perfect use of the theory of two-sided markets, let consumers perceive card payments as free lunch, because they paid no transaction fees and hardly any fixed (monthly or annual) fees, merchants were burdened with high costs of card acceptance. For those that had already begun accepting cards, there was no way out. They found themselves in a classical must-take-card trap. Meanwhile, those merchants that never started to accept cards (in particular small merchants) felt reluctant to change their attitude towards card payments due to their price elasticity against card charges. No wonder that falling interchange fees, resulting in lower merchant service charges, spurred growth in card acceptance network and, in turn, card usage through a self-reinforcing indirect network effect (externality). It is easier to identify this mechanism in those economies where merchant card acceptance was far from complete. Indeed, Australia and the USA were in a bit different situation than Poland, Spain or Italy before the reductions in interchange fees. In the former group of countries, stimulating card acceptance through lower merchant fees was never the regulators' chief motivation for intervention in the card payment market. However, it would be an obvious mistake to claim that lower card merchant fees did not contribute to the decision about installing a card payment acceptance device in those countries. Actually, in Australia it seems there is some confirmation for this phenomenon in statistics as well. In the USA, this aspect could be investigated in more detail. Furthermore, it needs to be remembered that this country is the birthplace and the stronghold of card schemes. The card payment acceptance network in the USA had been growing for decades already before Reg-II came into force.

All regulated markets experienced growth in card usage. Australia benefitted in particular from the intensified debit card usage, which has to be seen as a step towards a desired market outcome, in line with recommendations from studies on social costs of payment instruments, carried out by central banks. Also in Poland, at the time of interchange fee reforms, debit cards gained slightly relative to credit cards, although it is difficult for them to take away more market share from credit cards, because they already dominate strongly in the number and value of card transactions. Debit cards are socially more cost-efficient than credit cards and, above a specific transaction value threshold (different thresholds for different markets), more cost-efficient than cash. Therefore, development of debit cards is more desired that development of credit cards, which are more profitable for banks but, at the same time, less cost-efficient socially. American and Spanish regulations were followed by more intense credit card usage relative to debit card usage, which can be regarded as a downside of the reforms. This change was caused, among others, by the reverse competition, i.e. higher interchange fees applicable to credit cards than to debit cards, making issuance of the former more profitable for banks. In the USA, credit card interchange fees were not regulated at all, in Spain they were. The US banks were successful in incentivising credit card usage through reward programmes and adequate terms and pricing policy for credit and debit cards and checking or savings accounts. In Spain, consumers, facing higher annual credit card fees, valued the indirect network effect stemming from the growing card acceptance base more than they cared about higher annual credit card fees. In Australia, reverse competition gave Visa and Mastercard debit cards an edge over the domestic debit card system.

Regarding the monetary effects of the reductions in interchange fees, there are a few lessons to be drawn from all country cases studied with regard to both transmission channels: acquirer → merchant → consumer and issuer → consumer. Asymmetry of information, market frictions and the degree of competition within issuer, acquirer and merchant markets do matter. It is obvious that issuers try to keep the card revenues high and recover the income lost on lower interchange fees. Acquirers attempt to keep higher margins and not to pass lower interchange fees on merchants in the form of lower merchant service charges. Merchants would love to keep savings from lower interchange fees for themselves and not to share those savings with consumers. However, the studies show that most often market forces are working efficiently when there is a real competition game in place, meaning competition for lower prices/fees rather than for higher fees, as in the case of reverse competition.

In all countries, as a result of interchange fee reforms, issuers reduced card rewards and made it more challenging for cardholders to avoid fees but, perhaps with the exception of the USA, banks were rather unsuccessful in raising overall card- and account-holder fees permanently. Even though there were some leading and lagged effects, with issuers found to have introduced a non-linear pricing menu and fee increases, in the end, their significance for consumers was small or close to nil. In Australia, the fees were increased temporarily, if at all (see the doubts of the central bank of Australia) and then they fell, judging by the fluctuations in the fee-based banking income. In Poland, the net fee income fell seven times out of eight, comparing half-year periods and decreased by a considerable amount between 2012 and 2016 (see Sect. 3.4 for details). The increase in the fee income for the Polish banking sector in the second half of 2014 was small in magnitude compared to the fee-based income reductions over the three- or four-year period studied and to (actual and opportunity) gains from lower merchant fees. In Spain, per-transaction issuer revenues decreased, but total card revenues increased due to the compensation effect of the higher transaction number and value (see claim 4 from area 2).

In all countries studied, falling interchange fees were transferred effectively into lower merchant fees. With respect to the pass-through rate, the Polish case is instructive. Large merchants with IF+ or IF++ transparent merchant service charge (MSC) setting benefitted soon after interchange fee reductions became effective. On the other hand, what merchant surveys made apparent, small and medium-sized merchants subject to blended merchant rates later reaped benefits, on average, owing to the asymmetry of information and natural tendency of acquirers to keep higher margins as long as possible, that is as long as the competition in the acquiring market allowed it. The pass-through of the savings from lower interchange fees from acquirers to merchants was spread over time. Based on that fact, the pass-through of the corresponding savings from merchants to consumers had to be spread over time as well and depended on the competition in the merchant market. The cases studied do not yield straightforward evidence for lower prices of goods and services. Econometric modelling faces difficulties in isolating the effect of interchange fees for price setting from other factors which are much stronger in magnitude in this respect. This area can be further explored in future research. However, there are no reasons to contradict the economic theory. Business costs of merchants are reflected in prices. Even if there are doubts whether prices fall directly in reaction to falling merchant service charges, and there are some indications that retailers manage temporarily to keep savings for themselves, it is not conceivable and possible over longer time horizon. Business margins are shaped by the long-term competition in each sector of the industry. Lower interchange fees, rather than making prices fall, must contribute to lower rates of price increases (see claim 3 from area 1 and the Reserve Bank of Australia estimations). Furthermore, interchange fee reductions not only produce direct savings, which have just been discussed, but they also create considerable opportunity gains amounting to billions of AUD, USD, PLN, etc. These gains (savings) can be calculated by comparing the actual market scenario with the scenario in which interchange fees stay unchanged at the pre-reform level. Such calculations were made by the Reserve Bank of Australia, American researchers and by the author for Poland (see Chapters 2 and 3).

One could wonder whether in that alternative scenario where regulators do not intervene in the payment market and interchange fees remain high, the payment markets may benefit from more innovation, higher security of payments and less fraud. Such line of thinking seems to be flawed and not justified by the economic reality. High interchange fees were used to extract monopoly rents. The impact assessment for the interchange fee reforms studied makes it clear that neither innovation nor security of payments have been impaired by the caps on interchange fees. Innovation and security developments in Visa and Mastercard ecosystems have flourished. In recent years, tokenisation and Host Card

Emulation services, behavioural and biometric authentication solutions have emerged or advanced on the payment markets. Worldwide contactless (NFC) payments have boomed. Hardware and software investments in these areas are easily visible in Australia, the USA, Poland or Spain. Four-party schemes' strategic cooperation with BigTech companies has resulted in the expansion of mobile payments based on mobile wallets, such as: Apple Pay, Google Pay, Samsung Pay. The four-party card schemes' market position has not yet been deteriorated in any of the countries, although temporarily they lost some market share to three-party schemes in Australia or to some single-message networks in the USA. In the end, some time after the interchange fee reforms, Visa and Mastercard appeared to be even stronger. Their market share, market valuation and financial results support this claim.

No hard evidence has been found for major changes in the level of scheme fees for acquirers in Poland, but they are not investigated for other countries studied, due to lack of data, except for the acquirer (and issuer) US debit card network fees. Acquirer scheme fees are carefully scrutinised for the Polish case at the time of the reforms and later until 2018. Visa and Mastercard have revised and restructured the scheme (marketing and processing) fees but, more or less, their aggregate level for domestic payments has remained the same. Of course, the volume of payments has increased, with a positive impact on card schemes' profits. In order to falsify claim 5 from area 3 of the framework for assessing the impact of interchange fee reforms and to analyse more in-depth whether payment organisations put in place any rebalancing mechanism between acquirers and issuers as a result of the interchange fee reductions, it would be necessary to obtain non-public data on actual cash flows from acquirers and issuers to payment organisations. According to the evidence from the USA, however, where the FED gathers such data with regard to debit cards, the circumvention of that type has not been identified but, on the other hand, acquirer network fees have increased more compared to issuer network fees. Thus, in all likelihood, acquirer margins on debit card payments must have shrunk.

Beyond all shadow of doubt, Visa and Mastercard derive substantial benefits from strong network effects and the lock-in situation resulting from the global scale of activity, but both schemes experience a growing competition pressure due to: abolished or softened "honour-all-cards" and "no-surcharge" rules, restrictions on network exclusivity arrangements and network priority routing, separation of scheme and processing entities (EU), and falling interchange fees. Concerning the last one, reductions in interchange fees cause issuing banks to care more about the costs of operating Mastercard and Visa card payments. Therefore, they look for cost optimising strategies and become more open to new payment instruments (see claim 5 from area 3). There is a proof for that in Poland, where Inkart card authorisation and clearing system and the Blik mobile payment system were established coinciding with the timing of interchange fee reforms. Moreover, in all countries studied and everywhere in the world Visa's and Mastercard's position is challenged by innovative developments in real-time credit transfer payments and blockchain-enabled bitcoin and other alternative cryptocurrency payments. Apart from that, domestic card systems in different countries pose a competition threat, too (e.g. Chinese UnionPay or French *Cartes Bancaires*). Mastercard and Visa try to adapt to the FinTech revolution by setting up hubs and accelerator programmes where they take advantage of innovative ideas. They also invest in payment start-ups and acquire stakes in promising payment service providers and clearing houses (e.g. Visa's investment in Klarna from Sweden or Mastercard's investment in VocaLink from the UK). However, there is strong potential in the disruptive blockchain technology, altcoins, and, above all, in instant payments using simple credit transfers (see, for example, SCT inst in Europe, Bizum in Spain, Zelle in the USA, Blik and Express Elixir in Poland) to make four-party schemes obsolete or, at least, to seriously undermine their position. Also, the development of application programming interfaces (APIs) will leave an imprint on the payments landscape. The Unified Payments Interface is already extensively used in India and takes away payment flow from Visa and Mastercard card systems. The same is to be expected in Europe when, following the implementation of the second Payment Services Directive (PSD2), APIs will become fully operational, enabling functional payment initiation services based on credit transfers. In accordance with the PSD2, banks will have to open up to third-party providers in September 2019 at the latest.

It is not an easy task to regulate interchange fees and card payments. The impact of regulation needs to be assessed and monitored on an ongoing basis. Even if the reforms bring the desired outcome, as it was shown in the book, there is always a possibility that something can go wrong, as in the case of excessive surcharging in Australia, which was incidental but, still, existed. Effective as of 2019, Australian amendments to the Competition and Consumer Act 2010 will ensure that surcharging is limited to the costs of acceptance. Similar provisions have applied in the European Union according to the Consumer Rights Directive since 2012, but since January 2018, in accordance with the PSD2, merchants in the European Union have no longer been allowed to add any extra charge to the price of goods and services supplied to consumers paying with cards subject to the interchange fee caps. Unfortunately, regulators do not always resist the pressure from some stakeholders and withdraw from efficient transparency measures such as the full abolishment of NSR or HACR. On the other hand, restrictions on NSR and HACR are most often in force in jurisdictions which decided to regulate card payments. It should be emphasised that the right to surcharge card transactions does not necessarily lead to widespread surcharging (see, e.g. Poland where surcharging has always been rare). What it does is it improves the bargaining power of merchants against acquirers and leaves them the choice to change the business model, from the one exploiting the theory of two-sided markets, into one with transparent pricing reflecting the cost differences in accepted payment instruments. In addition, improving the access to four-party schemes by banning discriminatory licencing regimes (see, for example, the EU or Australia), prohibiting network exclusivity arrangements (see USA) or ensuring an easy identification of cards at the payment terminal (see EU and Australia)—all this has a positive effect on the competition in the card and payment market.

The lesson to be learned from the countries that have regulated interchange fees is that the reforms should rather be designed in a way to leave little room for circumventing the regulation. As the USA case shows, it was probably not the best decision to leave credit card interchange fees outside the regulation and to just cap debit card interchange fees. In Australia, capping weighted average interchange fee rates, instead of all rates uniformly, like in the EU, resulted in the proliferation of interchange fee categories and a cumbersome interchange fee structure overall. In the European Union, the potential loophole lies in leaving business cards outside the Interchange Fee Regulation's scope. The EU Regulation is at the moment the most complex one of all the regulations in the world. On the other hand, a question arises about the effectiveness and potential problems with some issues, e.g. with separating scheme from processing entities. Relevant provisions were implemented, not without a hitch, with substantial delay from the entry into force of the EU Interchange Fee Regulation. The other issue involves regulating three-party schemes as de facto four-party schemes with a hidden interchange fee mechanism. The practical question, however, is: where is the boundary line and should licencing partners be always treated as the party turning the three-party into a four-party scheme. It will be interesting to see in mid-2019 the results of the impact assessment carried out under the aegis of the European Commission for the European Economic Area, which is mandatory under the Interchange Fee Regulation review clause.

According to the theory of two-sided markets, the recipe for increasing the indirect network effect is taking advantage of different price elasticity of two groups of users. It has proven successful in various sectors of the economy, including the card industry, supporting the global expansion of Visa and Mastercard networks. However, the closer card acceptance is to being complete, the more concerns emerge about the rationale behind this business model. Moreover, other payment instruments, not included in this business model, e.g. cash or credit transfers, can be considered discriminated against. For the sake of efficient competition between payment instruments, it would be recommended to have transparent cost-based pricing in place where payers can compare costs of payment methods and make a conscious and price-driven choice.

Bibliography

Interchange Fee Regulation (EU) 2015/751 of the European Parliament and of the Council of 29 April 2015 on Interchange Fees for Card-Based Payment Transactions, OJ EU L 123/1.

Payment Services Directive (EU) 2015/2366 of the European Parliament and of the Council of 25 November 2015 on Payment Services in the Internal Market (PSD2), OJ EU L 337/35.

Index

J. Górka, *Interchange Fee Economics*,
https://doi.org/10.1007/978-3-030-03041-4

R

Printed by Printforce, the Netherlands